PERSONALITY
AND
CHRISTIAN FAITH

PERSONALITY AND CHRISTIAN FAITH

LOWELL G. COLSTON
&
PAUL E. JOHNSON

ABINGDON PRESS
nashville   new york

PERSONALITY AND CHRISTIAN FAITH

Copyright © 1972 by Abingdon Press

ISBN 0-687-30794-5

Library of Congress Catalog Card Number: 79-172815

MANUFACTURED BY THE PARTHENON PRESS AT
NASHVILLE, TENNESSEE, UNITED STATES OF AMERICA

PREFACE

Our purpose in this book is twofold: (1) to acknowledge and affirm the contemporary revolution in personal consciousness and to contribute in some measure to it; (2) to reaffirm our view that Christian faith, in spirit and by intent, is a potential source of vitality and perspective for that revolution. We say this in spite of an awareness that the revolt, in some aspects, is directed against ways in which the church has been guilty of repressing rather than liberating the human spirit.

The cultural situation which has triggered off the revolution and the dynamics of responses emerging as proposed changes, are the subjects of such recent popular books as Charles Reich's *The Greening of America* and Alvin Toffler's *Future Shock*. These books are notable among a number that are stirring the consciousness of people to an awareness of the meaning and direction of cultural change.

Reich, for example, writes perceptively of a new level of personal consciousness which is coming as a successor to that consciousness generated by an industrial society. It is characterized as an affirmation of selfhood which says, in effect, "I am glad I am me." (We may add a twist to that by appending, "and me I will surely be!")

With less hang-ups over guilt and anxiety, people are seen as getting in touch with themselves, honestly and appropriately. Along with this feeling goes a deep sense of personal responsibility for social welfare as well as a joyous and creative community life.

5

Toffler deals with the "shock" we experience confronting the future in every moment of our present existence. We are so overwhelmed by the rapidity and totality of change that we are not prepared to cope with it. He observes: "We can begin our battle to prevent shock at the most personal level." We can do this by bringing into consciousness ways of adapting to cultural changes which have largely been left to unconscious methods. Toffler sees this happening through conscious efforts to develop personal strategies to minimize human damage and increase personal capacities to cope with cultural change.

We are concerned with the theme which is central to both those books, although they are written from points of view which differ somewhat from each other and from our own. That theme we are identifying as creative potentiality in expanding personal consciousness, which, when actualized, gives vitality and stability to the emerging culture.

Presenting a model for the creative person, Charles Hampden-Turner, in his book *Radical Man*, suggests that the main theme to which we see ourselves contributing in this book is also basic to a dialogue between cultures. He calls for linking concepts to draw individuals into new relatedness in which the concerns of East and West may move toward a creative unity instead of division and enmity. We hope that such creative unity of world cultures may be sought in practical as well as theoretical ideals.

It seems to us that the clergyman is in a key position in the community for initiating and fostering such dialectical engagement. As highly developed individuals, laymen are also effecting the cooperation which is reaching out toward a larger, creative one world. The best hope for survival and meaning is in vigorous dialectic out of which mutuality and cooperation can come.

We are indebted to our colleague, Dr. Clark Williamson, professor of theology, Christian Theological Seminary, for valuable insights into contemporary theology.

We wish to give special thanks to members of our staff and

families whose encouragement and assistance have sustained us through proximate and remote labors together in preparing the manuscript. We are grateful to Becky Haycock, who helped us in typing the material; Sue Cardwell, administrative assistant in the area of pastoral care, who has carried many responsibilities in assisting us with the manuscript; Evelyn Johnson and Frances Colston, our respective wives whose support and help has been constant.

Lowell G. Colston
Paul E. Johnson

June 7, 1971

CONTENTS

Two: *Expansion of Personal Consciousness*

Three: *Consciousness and Faith*

One: Revolution in Personal Consciousness

I
Introduction

Alienation is a deep and fundamental problem of modern man. Alienation is the deadening of man's sensitivity to man. Maurice Friedman, in his book *The Problematic Rebel*, sees the problem of modern man as alienation resulting from the divided nature, the unresolved tension between personal freedom and psychological compulsion which follow on the death of God![1] Feeling unsupported by his faith, modern man experiences fragmentation in every area of his existence. We affirm with Theodore Roszak that "the revolution which will free us from alienation must be primarily therapeutic in character and not merely institutional."[2] Note that we did not say *not* institutional. We are quite aware of the valid claims of those who wish to change institutional structures, and we support them when we are convinced of their validity.

However, the answers to modern man's problems will not come in changing social structures alone, although such changes are inevitable and of great consequence. The need for changes lies deeper than institutional structures. It is to that need we are addressing ourselves in this book.

Modern man is so mesmerized by the prevailing scientific world view, he can hardly get out of it or beyond it sufficiently to be properly critical of it. He knows only that he is experienc-

[1] (Chicago: University of Chicago Press, 1970), see chapter 20, pp. 452-93.
[2] *The Making of a Counter-Culture* (Garden City, N. Y.: Doubleday, 1969), p. 97.

15

ing alienation from himself, from others, and from his environment. He looks to the system for the explanation of what has gone wrong. He not only does not find answers there, he actually compounds the problem. He even risks self-annihilation by the very technological juggernaut he is creating. He exploits the environment and becomes sad when he can no longer enjoy it. He exploits people and fosters deep chasms in the society, which he assumes would not be if everyone would become like himself. This is technocratic man of whom we are speaking.

He wrests power from the environment, then threatens to poison that environment with his noxious wastes. Despite his alarm at the obvious danger signals, he cannot help recognizing he has difficulty controlling his urge to control. Desperately in need of a changed perspective, the best he can offer is changed "structures" which emanate from his scientistic presuppositions.

Even the vigorous protests against various forms of domination of persons and groups through dehumanizing and depersonalizing technical controls do not stem from critical attacks upon the world view. Instead the cry seems to be, "You have what we want, and we will not be satisfied until we get it—at least, our share of it." Changing the structures to ensure an equitable distribution of the "fruits" of a technological society does not get at the more serious ills of our society.

We do not agree with the fundamentally pessimistic views of man espoused by either the New Left, with whatever shades of reinterpretation the modern followers of Karl Marx give them, nor their vociferous enemies, the extreme rightists, represented in great part by fundamentalist religious groups. As to their basic assumptions, they make strange bedfellows, indeed! Neither really are concerned with questioning the scientific world view which both take for granted. Their differences lie in their bitter quarrels over which group or groups can really be trusted to control the tools of a technocratic society. No doubt they each are fighting in the other what they deeply distrust in themselves. But the real question of how any of us can live in a world fragmented by the very scientific artifacts we extol is hardly considered.

We see the poignantly determinative revolution of our time as concerned with actualizing the profoundly personal potentialities in contemporary life. In fact, we see the proper endeavor of the present moment as a "both-and" process. Both man's social inventiveness and his personal creativity flow from an expanded consciousness.

Strange as may sound the idea of "expanding consciousness" through breaking out of the scientific world view, this is precisely what we mean. Modern man's love affair with "objective consciousness" has produced the obsequious "benefits" of starry-eyed, single-minded devotion to norms and values validated by it. He is charmed by the thrilling whirr of computers which calculate his existence with unerring, impassioned precision.

We find ourselves in basic agreement with Roszak's brilliant critique of the technocratic society from the point of view of its "youthful opposition." He observes:

A discerning few . . . have a shrewd sense of where the technocracy leaves off and the New Jerusalem begins: not at the level of class, party, or institution, *but rather at the non-intellective level of the personality from which these political and social forms issue* .[Italics ours.] They see, and many who follow them find the vision attractive, that building the good society is not primarily a social, but a psychic task. What makes the youthful disaffiliation of our time a cultural phenomenon, rather than merely a political movement, is the fact that *it strikes beyond ideology to the level of consciousness*, seeking to transform our deepest sense of the self, the other, the environment.[3]

The discovery of our deepest selves, and our undeniable interdependency with others and our environment, is the key to opening up the strongbox into which we have locked ourselves with our technical genius.

We should make clear at this point that we do not regard our view as anti-intellectual or even anti-scientific. When we affirm the "nonintellective" level, we speak of the vital and

[3] *Ibid.*, p. 49.

vast energies of the spirit which well up from the feeling level of man—a part of himself he often denies. In fact, we are calling for a spirited intellectualism integral to a spirited feeling—a rich blend of the subjective and objective consciousness. We reject reductionistic humanistic positions which corral persons and place them into intellectualistic and robotistic straitjackets.

We do not see our stance here as compatible with views based upon an individualistic ethos. We reject the moralistic presuppositions upon which such ethics are based. Therefore, we deny that we are advocating a form of modern pietism, although we are quick to state that there is much in pietism which is valid for contemporary man. The mutuality of pastoral care is a notable example. However, we are not as much interested in producing "good" individuals as in freeing people to become genuine and creative persons. The moralistic implications of "goodness" have historically come out practically as reductionistic modes of living.

Liberated persons are, by definition, unique and different from each other. In order to live together they learn to negotiate their differences. They engage in transactions which affirm and support their differences. We are aware that "changed" persons do not automatically produce changed institutions, but we believe that persons with expanding consciousness and greater awareness of their inner life will give greater impetus and vitality to institutions.

Dealing with the psychic as well as the social dimensions of issues gets at the tendency of the social activist to be secure in the belief that his manipulation of persons to whom he may not even be particularly sensitive is *prima facie* justified. The basic issues deriving from the uncontested world view may actually be obscured in the process. From that point of view the "change agent" is no more vindicated than those he is trying to change.

Violence feeds on the extreme forms of the contemporary protest for the very reason we have indicated. Contending that any domination is per se evil, the resisters of contemporary systems of control feel justified in using any means to destroy those systems. The tragic fallacy in their approach is that they are trying to fight fire with fire (to use an old, well-worn cliché), a basic inconsistency which is self-defeating in two ways: (1) Reactionaries tighten up their counterresistance and turn the events into propaganda to support their claims to control and dominate. (2) Critical dimensions of the issues involved become obscured in the battle for control of the instruments of the technical society. The human values for which legitimately they began the fight are lost in the struggle! What choice is there, then, between the causes of the combatants? Are there any real options? Or do we just exchange Scylla for Charybdis?

Those who argue for more control do so in the name of the virtues of the technical society to which they have "sold their birthrights for a mess of pottage." They cite examples of "more of this" and "better than that" as self-validating claims for the technical utopia in which they perceive themselves to live. The fact that many people get the life squashed out of them and are reduced to feelingless automatons is a matter of little consequence, since their situation is actually a historical necessity. "The poor will always be with us" is less a social commentary than it is the rather sobering reflection of powerless mechanistic pawns. What about the poor in spirit? Will they always be with us?

Alienation is truly overcome as people learn to live together in communities which liberate persons and facilitate personal growth. We say both liberate and facilitate, because the latter literally means "to make easy," whereas liberation is rarely, if ever, an easy matter. In fact, liberation involves jolting people out of delimiting, relatively unconscious modes of existence. Facilitation of movement toward expanding personal consciousness comes through group concern and support. People are enabled to grow by the caring community which supports that growth.

The Christian community is intentionally and potentially such a liberating and facilitating community for persons.

Whether it is true to that intention in any of its particular concrete expressions depends wholly on whether it is sensitive to the spirit of its own kerygma. There are many indications that the early Christian community interpreted its *raison d'être* precisely in these terms.

In each of his letters to the various churches, the apostle Paul takes some occasion to emphasize the liberating intent of the gospel. He wrote to the Galatians: "For freedom Christ has set us free; stand fast therefore, and do not submit again to a yoke of slavery" (Gal. 5:1). Continuing the theme, he admonishes them: "For you were called to freedom, brethren; only do not use your freedom as an opportunity for the flesh, but through love be servants of one another" (Gal. 5:13).

Seeking to set a style of life appropriate to a liberating and facilitating community, Paul addressed the Ephesians as follows: "Therefore, putting away falsehood, let every one speak the truth with his neighbor, for we are members one of another. Be angry but do not sin; do not let the sun go down on your anger, and give no opportunity to the devil" (Eph. 4:25). Paul was clearly noting how grudge-bearing and the harboring of resentment ultimately wreak evil consequences in the lives of those affected by such reactions.

These are but a few examples of Paul's views on the meaning of the Christian gospel. Essentially he was saying people should be set free from whatever dominated them, whether it be their own passions, negative emotions ("the law of sin and death"), political powers ("neither principalities nor powers), or whatever denied a man his true freedom.

Also Paul cautioned against easy adaptations of the gospel to particular world views, which tended to justify an existing style of life. He warned the Colossians, for example, of the self-debasement fostered by the mystery cults which attracted the people who were largely fascinated by being mystified, although they did not understand what they were experiencing. "Therefore, since Jesus was delivered to you as Christ and Lord, live your lives in union with him," he said. "Be rooted in him; be built in him; be consolidated in the faith you were taught; let your hearts overflow with thankfulness." (Col. 2:6-7 NEB.)

The acts of liberation and facilitation are acts of grace. They come from "hearts overflowing with thankfulness." We have been encountered, instructed and supported by people who have cared enough for us to give unstintingly of themselves to us. No possible price for repayment can be exacted or is expected. The great measure of gratitude which the "saints" felt was passed on in the form of responsible and loving care and service. Such is the nature of the Christian community when it is being true to itself.

We see Christian faith as essentially liberating in that it is generated from central belief in the loving, self-giving character of God. This belief has been under constant, unrelenting attack from many quarters for some time. To the degree that the church has lost or has compromised its prophetic stance and action in exposing and breaking up the power-grabbing and status-maintaining techniques of persons or groups who dominate others, it invites such attack. The instigators of the criticism perceive the gross inconsistency in ascribing the terms *loving* and *self-giving* to a tyrannical God who seems bent on satisfying basically insecure and neurotic needs to control rather than to trust and "love people into being."

The person's view of God and the world shapes his views of himself and those around him. If the world is a great machine to be comprehended and manipulated, then the people in it become objects to be understood and controlled. Rather than letting them speak out of their essence (or enjoying any of the environment for what it is in itself), we look at them through our distorted mechanistic lenses and see what we want to see. It is true, as often contended, that responsible scientists have exploded myths. However, myths are not bad because they are myths, but because they are "bad" myths; and they are bad myths because they promote what the transactional analysts have called "Not-O.K." feelings about other people.

When systems support the "you are not O.K." attitudes, they no longer engender true human values. Thus they must be changed to become "servants" rather than "masters." We believe this was the central message of the Christian kerygma from its very beginning. The servant role was regarded as the prototype for all personal and community self-images. However, the servant role was not regarded as servile, in the weak sense, but service in the strong sense. A person is not called to foster dominance by giving in to it—on the contrary, by challenging it with the stronger force of faithful self-giving.

A definition of personality which serves as the basis for our discussion is: *Personality is the dynamic mutual interaction of all systems which comprise and affect the organism.* Among these systems are physical, social, economic, political, ecological, etc., which are held together in a total organization known as *personality.*

Gordon Allport has observed, "The best hope for discovering coherence would seem to lie in approaching personality as a total functioning structure, i. e., as a *system.* To be sure, it is an incomplete system, manifesting varying degrees of order and disorder. . . . And yet personality is well-enough knit to qualify as a system—which is defined merely as *a complex of elements in mutual interaction.*" [4]

We feel that this interpretation is valid and helpful, but falls short of giving the whole story. We maintain that the personality as system, in the sense Allport has seen it, exists among systems which critically affect and make it up. Therefore, we believe that personality cannot be adequately conceptualized apart from a consideration of these systems. Or, to put it positively, personality is the total organization of systems.

For example, a medical model of healing which concentrates on the sick individual must not be construed as the whole. Treating the person and returning him to a sick environment is actually a kind of patchwork approach. Obviously when the person becomes ill, emergency measures are required. Medical science has made tremendous and responsible contributions to the treatment of the ill. However, the physician who assumes

[4] *Pattern and Growth in Personality* (New York: Holt, Rinehart and Winston, 1961), p. 567.

that what he is doing comprises the whole of what is required to aid and abet the healing process is simply not showing awareness of the true complexity of wholeness!

Systems which affect every person—economic, political, ecological, etc.—have as much to do with shaping the personality as the organism's own internal structures. Likewise, a powerful person has a profound effect upon those systems. Effective mutual transactions can take place if the energies of the body are liberated and the imagination set free for the fashioning of systems conducive to liberating all of the energies and potentialities of people.

Energies for the transformation needed in both personal and community forms of existence are coming from the contemporary revolution in personal consciousness. We are saying we see the revolt as being against mechanistic interpretations of the person which have tended to put the lid on his possibilities and caused us to settle for far less for too long.

In this book we wish to add our support to those who are earnestly calling for a stirring of personal consciousness. We believe the Christian gospel speaks to the alienated condition of man, that it affirms the values of personal creativity and responsibility as prerequisites to healing his estrangement.

II

The Person in Changing Perspectives

There are many ways of seeing a person from one point of view or another. What is man? He is lord of creation, made in the image of God with infinite potentialities. He is a worm of the dust, and to the dust he will return. He is a hairless ape. He is a synthesis of chemicals worth $1.79. He is an enemy to destroy before he destroys us. He is a machine operator, a robot to keep the wheels of industry turning. He is a black man rising in holy wrath against his oppressors. He is another kind to be stripped and consumed in the gas chambers. Yet he has power to mount a revolution and change the world.

What is woman? She is a vision of divine beauty and heavenly love. She is the handmaiden of her master. She is the mother of our children. She is the tender trap to hold man by her seductive charms. She is the house slave who chases dirt and children while the man goes free to seek his fortune in the larger world. She is the customer lured by fashion designers and courted by advertisers. She is the office secretary who does her work with a smile and radiates a gracious spirit in the reception room. She is a sister of mercy who nurses the sick, teaches the young, and cares for the aged. She is an ardent worker for peace and justice, health and welfare. She is a voter who has potential power to change the course of history.

What is a child? She is a cherub who comes to us as a gift from heaven. He is a bed-wetting, thumb-sucking brat. She is a jolly playmate or a wailing crybaby. They are the population explosion. Yet a growing person is eager to learn and develop from one step to the next. A young person is bursting with potentialities. He falls madly in love and prefers his own age group. He is going to be himself, choose his own mate and vocation, decide for himself. She is coming into the beauty of womanhood to be admired. She is to be protected and controlled before things get out of hand. What can you do with these long-haired radicals? Why do the young people want to change everything? Yet it is their world to shape as future parents and leaders.

It is evident that persons look very different according to the perspective from which we see them. Even the same person appears in a new light from another perspective. And our perspectives are constantly changing as we move around the person. We see this clearly when the television camera moves from side to side, or from a distant to a closeup view of the person in focus. Our first impression will be incredibly naïve when we come to know a person better. We actually choose where we stand to view other persons, even though we move in social perspectives of our kind.

1. Ways of Meeting a Person

If you are going to meet me on a street corner in the center of the city (let us say Meridian and Washington Streets), we will be looking for each other. As I come to the corner, I peer intently along the streets to see if I can identify you. I may be attracted by a distant outline, and study the style of clothing, the manner of walking, and the features by which to recognize you. If the streets are crowded, my eyes will dart rapidly from person to person in a persistent search for the one who is coming to meet me. And when we do recognize each other, there will be a wave, a smile, or some response drawing us together until we are near enough to speak and enter into conversation.

Meeting a person is no simple act, but a complicated process of many steps and transactions. The crowding stream of other

25

persons who pass me with no sign of recognition are not engaged in the intricate event of meeting. They are avoiding me
as an obstacle in their way, observing my position and direction to escape collision and move on to other goals. To them
I am no more than an object to miss, a thing blocking their
onward course. The meaning of my life to them is reduced to
a minimum in which nothing of my unique personhood cap-
tures their concern except to get by me as quickly as possible.
If no one is meeting me as a person, I become a nonentity in
that context, an It or shadowy form that calls forth no concern
or responsibility to be something more together.

The event of meeting a person is far more exciting than
passing by a human object. I bring to you an alert awareness
of what you are—man or woman, young or old, vital or weary,
neat or disheveled, expressive or deadpan. And I care enough
to wonder who you are, why you are coming this way, and
where you are going. Observing comes to sharper focus in a
searching for the meaning of this person and a reaching out
toward relationship.

As we respond in these ways to each other, person to person,
we are drawn together into a sphere of common life. Looking
directly to each other, eyes meet in mutual interest, faces are
mobile and expressive, we smile or nod even as strangers who
acknowledge the other's presence. We may then move toward
each other to introduce ourselves and begin to speak. This is
a fateful step, for otherwise we pass by to conclude the incident
and avoid a further relationship. To speak in passing is a well-
known custom in a community where we affirm the right of
the other person to be here too. Such recognition is a signal
of mutual trust, which is the basic requirement of a community. Yet passing by indicates, "Keep your distance; do not
trespass on my time or privacy. We have greeted each other;
let us be minding our own business."

At any rate we meet by moving from observing to responding. If I am sitting on a park bench (observes Jean-Paul Sartre),
and a person seated at the other end of the bench looks at me,
I am not the same as I was before. For when I know he has

26

looked at me, he has brought my attention to him and this puts a responsibility upon me. We are now both in the same world, and he has some claim upon me. What is he thinking about me? Why does he look at me? What interests him and what does he want? How do I feel toward him? Am I fearing him, wanting to avoid him and keep him away at a safe distance? Or do I feel interested enough to speak and let us know each other better?

This actually puts me in a dilemma where a choice is necessary. Shall I get up and walk away to keep a safe distance? Or shall I sit there pretending I have not noticed him? Shall I go on eating lunch or reading my book? Shall I look the other way as if absorbed in the birds and flowers? Or shall I respond to him by returning his gaze and begin to speak of "A nice day, isn't it"? This would presumably lead to further conversation, and we would be engaged in the larger dimensions of a meeting.

We might speak of neutral subjects carefully selected as safe and uninvolving. Or I could introduce myself and ask his name. If this should be the course of our conversation, we would be persons to each other, exchanging information as to who we are, where we live and work, what is important to us to oppose or affirm, how we feel, and what concerns us as we wrestle with the meaning and purpose of life. How long to continue the conversation is also a dilemma, and whether to part as strangers who separate for good, or to plan another meeting. If we plan to meet again, we face the question of our intentions. Where shall we meet, what shall we do, and what shall we mean to each other?

There was a time when Lowell Colston and Paul Johnson were unknown to each other. Eventually we heard of each other, came together at a national conference on clinical pastoral education, and served on its governing board. Though we were not intending to avoid each other, each saw and affirmed the other in a distant and rather formal way. Though both of us were teaching in the same field of personality and pastoral care at theological seminaries, we were a thousand miles apart.

It was not until 1965 that we were destined to know each other more deeply, when we began to work together as colleagues at Christian Theological Seminary and affiliated programs of continuing education for pastors. Since then our meetings have been more frequent and our dialogue continuous. We associate as families, relive our earlier years in Iowa, and consider our plans for the future. We participate with faculty and committees in designing education for the ministry in its many forms, explore theological and psychological issues, develop and supervise pastoral counseling services, conduct classes, all-day seminars and twelve-day workshops for pastors, enlist interdisciplinary teamwork with community leaders, churchmen, and groups who desire a united approach to understand and serve human life in truer perspective.

From the converging of these disciplines and the meeting of these persons, we enter this conversation with you on personality and Christian faith. We will need first to examine changing perspectives upon persons. To do so, we will offer a critique of what we consider to be reductionist views of man, which, of course, deeply affect interpretations of the meaning of persons. We intend to be fair with the scientists of man, acknowledging their contributions, while criticizing the technological assumptions upon which they have based their work. Many have been helpful in giving us insight into ourselves, but some have been delimited by their views of the world. A revolution is going on in the social sciences in an effort to be germane to the actualization of the person as he struggles within his turbulent social context.

2. The Sciences of Man

The sciences of man may be classified as biological, psychological, and social. Yet they overlap extensively to gain a larger perspective, and subdivide continuously to focus on ever finer microscopic details. The hermit scientist working alone in his attic like Spinoza is a heroic myth. The work of discovery and invention is a social process in which the community of scientists are in dynamic interaction with each other through a network of communication and publication. The authentic scientist is constantly studying the research of others to advance along well-marked frontiers. And he submits his own research to others for testing and verification. By such cooperation the acceleration of scientific knowledge is amazing, beyond the wildest dreams of those who lived before the twentieth century.

The biological sciences are multiplying until they represent a growing cluster of interrelating disciplines, which draw upon the entire reservoir of scientific theory and employ the intricate methods and instruments of every science. Mobilized by the goal of saving and enlarging health, the medical sciences are achieving spectacular results in tracing and guiding the course of micro-organisms and body chemistry to combat diseases, regulate the ova, and affect the entire interactive processes of life in vital balance.

To consider the future of these sciences is at once exhilarating and frightening. For knowledge is power, and we may wonder how well we will use the tremendous increase of power to control the life entrusted to us. Robert Sinsheimer, professor of biophysics at the California Institute of Technology, puts it this way:

How will you choose to intervene in the ancient designs of nature for man? Would you like to control the sex of your offspring? It will be as you wish. Would you like your son to be six feet tall? Seven feet? Eight feet? What troubles you? Allergy? Obesity? Arthritic pain? These will be easily handled. For cancer, diabetes, there will be genetic therapy. The appropriate DNA will be provided in the appropriate dose. Viral and microbial disease will be easily met. Even the timeless patterns of growth and maturity and aging will be subject to our design. How long would you like to live? . . . The foundation of ethics is foresight. But how can we predict the ultimate consequence of the alteration of ourselves? In all of science we have been in a sense children, spewing change into society with scant thought for the consequences.[1]

[1] Quoted by Robert M. Hutchins, "Doing What Comes Scientifically," *The Center Magazine*, II (January, 1969), 56.

Biologists are seeing that man is not a helpless victim of the evolutionary process, but able to direct and reshape that process. Now we are confronted by the consequences of our choice and our neglect. This ability to choose requires responsibility. Man "need not be a passive spectator, . . . for . . . he is an active participant in the process of creation. Here is the greatest challenge ever put to human thought and culture." [2] So speaks a professor of zoology.

Shall we play God? This question was asked by Leroy Augenstein, late chairman of biophysics at Michigan State University. After seeing the portentous responsibility of mind manipulation, organ transplants, the population explosion, the prevention of birth defects, and the extension of life, we must face up to the question: What is man? Why is he here? Augenstein concludes that we do play God when we spray a garden with pesticide, or when a surgeon picks up a scalpel to correct a physical defect. We exist because two people played God in creating life. Who will decide how we put our knowledge to work? "Only if many are willing to stand up and be counted will religion have much to say about controlling the quality of life and determining what man should be." [3]

A professor of sociology asks, What can man make of man? Today's advances in biology, especially in reshaping the genetic code and synthesizing life to new goals, will have revolutionary consequences. Who will be the trustees of these powers, and who will guard the guardians? No science can escape being a servant of society. Even though scientists may not claim to be experts in values, yet they must accept some responsibility for the use of their discoveries. We stand on the threshold of a major revolution in human history. We cannot turn the clock back nor entrust our future to vagaries of random cultural developments. For man as never before is shaping the world

[2] Theodosius Dobzhansky, "Evolution: Implications for Religion," in Kyle Haselden and Philip Hefner, eds., *Changing Man: The Threat and the Promise* (Garden City, N. Y.: Doubleday Anchor Books, 1969), p. 155.
[3] Leroy Augenstein, "Should We Play God?" *ibid.*, p. 99.

through his knowing and doing. Moral neutrality is a hazardous luxury.

If what is unique about man is his "personhood"—man as a self-conscious center of action—must we not incorporate this as a constant into our biotechnology? And how? . . . In this sense it is quite obvious that our works do not save us. . . . Here the affirmations of faith must count; and the kinds of communities of faith men belong to may be decisive.[4]

Our knowledge of man is growing through the work of the psychological sciences, which are also multiplying and clustering. The American Psychological Association in 1969 unites twenty-nine divisions of psychology, with thirteen journals reporting the scientific activities of its 28,785 members. If we remember the limited viewpoint of the founders of psychology less than a century ago, and the reductive determinism that has circumscribed a good part of its history, we may be astonished at the expansive sense of destiny, power, and freedom which characterizes the outlook of psychologists today.

"Shall Psychology 'Manage' Its Future?" is the title of the 1968 annual report of the executive officer, Arthur H. Brayfield.[5] Four influences are noted as giving rise to this question: (1) Psychology has become swept up in the practical affairs of man, and this calls for social responsibility. (2) Psychology has become an object of public interest, viewed by government as a national resource in reference to massive social problems such as war and peace. (3) The complexity and diversity of human affairs as influenced by modern science and technology have put a premium on systematic efforts at *future-planning*. (4) The educational and scientific estate of which psychology is a part is a "power center" in American life, and we will have to know what we are doing.

Obviously we have moved beyond the individual psychologist doing it on his own. We are a community within and responsi-

---

[4] Karl H. Hertz, "What Man Can Make of Man," *ibid.*, p. 111.
[5] *American Psychologist*, XXIII (December, 1968), 844-48.

ble to the larger community of man. Brayfield sums up the position of psychologists in 1968 in this way:

1. Those persons and institutions engaged in the production, communication, and use of psychological knowledge constitute a *dynamic system* in which events occurring in any one part are reflected in other elements of the system and ultimately in the performance of the discipline.

2. Psychologists have a continual responsibility to examine the operation of this system as it serves the needs of the science and of society, to understand the system and its functioning as completely as possible, and to exercise management over it within the limits set by such understanding and by the goals and resources of the discipline.[6]

Reviewing the significant work of task forces in the area of health services, services to children, minority groups, employment procedures, and jointly establishing the Behavioral and Social Sciences Survey Committee to appraise these expanding fields of knowledge, he concludes that "APA has moved from a reactive posture to an active stance . . . better equipped and more disposed to take the initiative." Psychiatry, by the interaction of biology and psychology, is coming to understand the conditions of mental health and by cooperation with the social sciences work toward social health in family and community. It seems as if there is a race among our scientists to raise the most profound ethical issues for society—whether to exploit and destroy or to create and enlarge the values of human life.

The social sciences are also involved in the race to understand and develop the hidden potentialities of every person in our whole society. The most pressing and crucial issues of our time, deeply affecting each individual, are the problems and possibilities of our relationships to each other. There can be no doubt that more attention should be focused on our social

[6] *Ibid.*, p. 845. The American Psychological Association recently announced a new Department of Social and Ethical Responsibility. The aim will be "to act as a clearing house and a locus for creative and innovative approaches to social responsibility for psychology." *APA Monitor* (Washington, D. C.) March, 1971, p. 1.

interdependence. For the satisfaction of each person's needs is mutually dependent upon the actions and attitudes of other persons. This is painfully evident in marital conflict, the generation gap, desegregation, riots, and international relations where explosive rivalries erupt in bitterness, war, and destruction.

In the proliferating cluster of the social sciences one focus is upon the larger structure of social institutions (sociology); another focus is upon political and economic movements shaping the life of mankind (political and economic sciences); another focus turns to the history and development of societies and cultures (history and anthropology); another focus is concerned with the interrelationships of organisms and their environment (ecology); another searches for the meaning of life together and the values to serve as the goals of human striving (social ethics). These are all extensive macrocosmic studies of social forces and movements in large perspective.

Social psychology is an intensive or microcosmic study of human life in the more intimate relationships of person to person within the face to face interactions of individuals and groups. The concern here is for the inner meaning of these relations to the person as he perceives his role and identity in response to the expectations of others. It is also concerned with interactive and dynamic influences of family, school, church, and the cultural norms of the community on the individual; with the behavior patterns and attitudes forming through these relationships.

There is a mood of fatalism in our time that we are caught as helpless pawns in the irresistible social forces of the great society. But this is not the conclusion of social psychologists and many other human scientists today. Social science began with a mechanistic view of man as a victim of evolutionary processes.[7] In the natural sciences man was viewed as actively gain-

[7] Gibson Winter shows the influence of Herbert Spencer (1820-1903) upon American sociologists and William Graham Sumner's view in his *Folkways* (1906) of man's helplessness before these social forces. See Gibson Winter, *A Social Ethic: Perspective on Social Process* (New York: Macmillan, 1966), p. 7.

ing control of his environment; yet in the early activity of the social sciences man was seen as a passive object of forces playing upon him.

This view is vigorously challenged by leading social scientists in their passionate debate over functionalism and voluntarism. Social scientists who have taken a neutral stance toward society are now challenged by the scientists who say we are already involved in the social process, and are therefore responsible for the course of our social movements. The functionalists trust the effectiveness of technology in transforming society, while the voluntarists call for intervention to shape the society of the future.[8] Functionalists see their role to describe society and let nature take its course; voluntarists call for responsible participation in the social process as agents of change.

In either case the social scientist is offered a choice and asked to decide how he will act as an informed person in reference to our society. Actually, man creates society, and he has some choice whether he will seek to change it or let it run its natural course. There is voluntarism in the freedom of each scientist to weigh the alternatives and decide how he will wrestle with the data of society and what he will do with these choices before him. Whatever model he constructs of man and society, even when he contends that the individual is helpless, is his choice. For he decides what he will construct in theory and how he will proceed in practice.

This is clearly acknowledged by George Herbert Mead, a pioneer functionalist, who said: "The individual is no thrall of society. He constitutes society as genuinely as society constitutes the individual." [9]

The rise of the term "individual" is questioned by Casserly, who points to it as an abstraction without historical reality.[10]

[8] *Ibid.*, p. 46.

[9] Mead, *Mind, Self and Society*, ed. Charles W. Morris (Chicago: University of Chicago Press, 1934), p. xxv.

[10] J. V. Langmead Casserly, *Morals and Man in the Social Sciences* (London: Longmans Green & Co., 1951), pp. 213-14. Quoted by Walter G. Muelder in his *Moral Law in Christian Social Ethics* (Richmond: John Knox Press, 1966), p. 40.

None of us have met any individuals, he says, for they do not exist. The term "person," however, is concrete and historical, alive and participating with other persons in the living community which is a continuing product of interpersonal relations.

Person and society are not natural enemies, as Freud saw it in *Civilization and Its Discontents* (1930). They are not truly antithetical, but mutually interdependent in the sense that neither can exist without the other. How can social science overlook the natural union of person and society? For persons are alive and interacting not as isolated individuals but as persons-in-relationship. They are not empty receptacles into which social culture is poured, but creative and responsive persons who seek to know and interact with others in a community of life interests and purposes.

3. Theological Perspectives of Man

In view of what we said earlier—that we do not intend to be anti-scientific in our approach—what is a proper stance as theologians? We have it strictly within our charge not to allow a scientific world view to tyrannize modern man to the point of rendering him impervious to his own psyche.

On the other hand, we should make clear at the outset of this disucssion that we find no eternal chasm or preconditions that set science and theology forever against each other. This may have been a plausible myth in the prescientific era of Galileo, when there was a single man against the pope, or a simple proposition upheld by a few dissenting scientists against a doctrine held by a council of church leaders to be infallible. But in this day of many diverse viewpoints and sciences on many frontiers debating or revising the work of others, there is no monolithic science in battle array; any more than one theological argument can be held as final truth against the wealth of diversity which many other theologians bring as revealing interpretations of man.

This separation of natural versus supernatural which was once taken for granted has been challenged since Bonhoeffer

35

as a symptom of a theological disease, which he called "thinking in two spheres." [11] To think in two spheres is to divide reality into a dichotomy of opposition. It has long been popular to reduce the complexity of the world into this oversimplified division, such as heaven/earth, light/darkness, good/evil, man/woman, sacred/secular. There is an interpenetrating unity among these dichotomies that denies such false separations. E *pluribus unum* is a truer concept—to see how the many are related in a larger wholeness, in which apparent bipolarity has a deeper unity not to be artificially separated. What we find on closer inspection is an organic pluralism of the many interacting in a dynamic and interdependent wholeness.

Yet there are boundaries to recognize among the various disciplines of our sciences and theologies, within which to constitute a system. The fallacy is to raise high walls of artificial separation, when in reality we must cross over these open boundaries if we are to comprehend and cooperate in the endless quest and utilization of true understanding. Every scientific hypothesis invites honest research, and every theological position calls for rigorous examination and debate to explore and draw out the complexities and countertendencies that characterize the mystery of human life.

Some theologians may oppose a scientific view, but it is not possible in our time for all theologians to oppose all scientists. Our world is too open for such walls to divide the life of our human community into sealed compartments. Actually every person in our world today is open to scientific thinking and participates more or less in the fruits of scientific discovery and invention. It is inevitable, therefore, that every theology of man will be in some ways conversant with and influenced by our scientific culture, which is so pervasive as to constitute, even unconsciously, the fabric of whatever views we may take of man.

[11] Dietrich Bonhoeffer, *Ethics*, ed. Eberhard Bethge (New York: Macmillan, 1955), pp. 196 ff. He continues: "There are not two realities, but only one reality, and that is the reality of God, which has become manifest in Christ in the reality of the world" (p. 197).

What do contemporary theologians say about the nature of man? We will call on those theologians who have been most concerned with the person in his future-seeking, social-relating, ever-creating, and self-transcending destiny. Teilhard de Chardin, Martin Buber, Paul Tillich, and Reinhold Niebuhr are among the few who have written explicitly on the subject. In brief outline let us note characteristic features of man which can be seen through the eyes of these representative theologians. These four themes which they portray are immediately relevant to our study of the person in changing perspectives.

1. *Man is a future-oriented being.* There can be no doubt that man is a historical being. But if he were only a creature of history, he would be caught in the web of the past like a fly unable to free himself from his doom. The tight nexus of these causal relationships uncovered by the sciences may seem to narrow the life space until we are ready to yield to despairing determinism. It is true the past has passed into history beyond recall; and yet the book of history is not closed, but open; we may learn from the lessons of the past, and from this perspective plan the future.

Teilhard de Chardin (1881-1955), Jesuit priest-scientist, explored geological time in the distant past, yet he devoted himself passionately to the future of man.[12] To those immobilists who insist that nothing moves, he replies the whole universe is moving, and we are moving too. Though the mountains seem firmly fixed in rigid form, the geologist finds the movement that shaped them is continuing slowly to reshape and change their future. The evolution of life, which seems to have arrived at fixed organic forms, is by no means finished, for all life is constantly changing. Growth is the most essential character of life.

There is a vast evolutionary process around us, in which all matter and organic life participate. Of all this change the most crucial alternatives come to focus in the sphere of consciousness. What is the difference, he asks, between ourselves as citi-

[12] See Teilhard de Chardin, *The Future of Man* (New York: Harper, 1964).

zens of the twentieth century and the earliest human beings? Organically the faculties of those remote ancestors were probably equal to our own.

The great superiority over Primitive Man which we have acquired and which will be enhanced by our descendants in a degree perhaps undreamed-of by ourselves, is in the realm of self-knowledge; in our growing capacity to situate ourselves in space and time, to the point of becoming conscious of our place and responsibility in relation to the Universe.[13]

Though our forefathers lived within the limited frame of a brief yesterday, in a small confine on a flat earth, supposing that each man contained within himself his own destiny, there came a dawning awareness of larger horizons. Until at last these close boundaries have melted away before the light of our expanding knowledge. The explosion of this new knowledge has blown these walls away in all directions, until the world is open to us on every side; and we come to see ourselves in the potentialities of larger infinities of space and time. We confront a boundless universe to which, in ways we had not known before, we are called to belong and join in a greater destiny in which we are to have a significant part.

At once humbled and ennobled by our discoveries, we are gradually coming to see ourselves as a part of vast and continuing processes; as though awakening from a dream, we are beginning to realise that our nobility consists in serving, like intelligent atoms, the work proceeding in the Universe. We have discovered that there is a Whole, of which we are the elements. We have found the world in our own souls.[14]

Teilhard insists this is not merely the establishment of an idealized system of extrinsic relationships. It is no intellectual luxury or curiosity to be satisfied. The consciousness of our relationship with the entire universe actually represents a genuine enlarging of our unique personalities. Yet this enlarging is only possible by the awareness of our relationships, in which

[13] *Ibid.*, p. 16.
[14] *Ibid.*, pp. 16-17.

we participate by a progressive realization of the universality of whatever surrounds each of us. This growing coextension of our soul and the world through awareness of these relationships is the natural outcome of an organic process arising from the germination of life and the growth of the brain, enabling us to perceive the meaning of this greatness and participate with others in moving toward a future yet dimly foreseen.

As Teilhard traces this progress from the prehuman to ultrahuman, he sees that man differs so little anatomically from other primates that he may be seen as no more than a minor offshoot. Yet in the biosphere man has ascended to a position of amazing leadership among other forms of life. This hominization of our planet is enveloping it before our eyes with a growing edge of thinking substance, which he calls the Noosphere (from *noos*, the mind).

This Noosphere becomes a new matrix of the whole human community, surrounding the newborn child, out of which he cannot be wrenched without mutilation, and by which the growing person is nourished and educated into a common humanity. Life in this Noosphere "cannot rebound in a new spring forward without acquiring a morality, and . . . a 'faith,' without becoming 'mysticized' . . . In Man evolution is interiorised and made purposeful." [15]

There is the crucial question whether this something ultrahuman is being born through socialization, or whether man can only attain it by rising vertically to a fuller life above the material zones of the world. Shall we put our faith in the upward or the forward? Here a modern religious crisis appears, a conflict of faith between the horizontal and vertical dimensions of life. Teilhard, as theologian and scientist in one, sees no final conflict here as he finds evolution coinciding with the incarnation of God in Christ.

The supernaturalising Christian Upward is incorporated (not immersed) in the human Forward. . . . Faith in God, in the very degree in which it assimilates and sublimates within its own spirit

[15] *Ibid.*, pp. 209, 212.

the spirit of Faith in the World, regains all its power to attract and convert.[16]

The whole future of the Earth, as of religion, seems to depend on the awakening of our faith in the future.[17]

Some religions teach the eternal recurrence of the past in endless cycles of repetition. The Bible, however, draws faith from the past and finds hope in the future. Judeo-Christian history marches steadily forward, affirming the work of God with men in the past and expectantly awaiting what he will do in the future. The Old Testament awaits the Messiah, and the New Testament claims the revelation of God in Christ who goes forward and upward into the unknown future, in the course of God's unfolding purpose.

Therefore, since we are surrounded by so great a cloud of witnesses, let us also lay aside every weight, and sin which clings so closely, and let us run with perseverance the race that is set before us, looking to Jesus the pioneer and perfecter of our faith, who for the joy that was set before him endured the cross, despising the shame, and is seated at the right hand of the throne of God. (Hebrews 12:1-2.)

2. *Man is a related being.* Whether we look to the past or the future we find persons becoming what they are through relationships. Historical theology sees man in relation to God. Future-oriented theology sees the destiny of man in relation to our expanding universe, where persons meet on a moving stage to play their part in ever new adventures. To know a person in the concrete wholeness of his multi-dimensional life, we must comprehend him in the full meaning of his relatedness. For every person is a related being.

An eloquent spokesman for this view of man is Martin Buber (1878-1965), one of the universal men whose influence upon our age is beyond calculation. His basic thesis is that real life is meeting, an encounter of person with person, a dialogue of address and response. Primary words do not refer to things,

[16] *Ibid.*, p. 268.
[17] *Ibid.*, p. 7.

or describe what might exist independently. Primary words are spoken from the being, and they indicate relations. One primary word is *I-Thou*, and this can only be spoken with the whole being. The other primary word is *I-It*, and it can never be spoken with the whole being.[18]

There is no *I* taken in itself, but only the I of the primary word *I-Thou* and the *I* of the primary word *I-It*.[19]
If I face a human being as my *Thou*, and say the primary word *I-Thou* to him, he is not a thing among things, and does not consist of things.[20]
The *Thou* meets me. But I step into direct relation with it. Hence the relation means being chosen and choosing, suffering and action in one; just as any action of the whole being.[21]

If a man is satisfied with the things he uses, he lives in the past. He has nothing but objects which subsist in time that has been. The present arises only when Thou becomes present. I come alive in the present when I acknowledge Thou.

Love is responsibility of an I for a Thou. . . . Love does not cling to the Thou for its object; but love is between I and Thou. . . . Hate is by nature blind. Only a part of a being can be hated.[22]

Is Buber speaking of the ultimate Thou, whom we call God, or of each person I meet on the road of life? He means both God and fellowman, for we do not find God by turning away from man. Rather God meets us on every road where we meet and reverence a person, whoever he may be. Yet if we scorn or use another person, we treat him as an object, *It*, and deny his thou-ness. He is present to us as Thou only as we respect and accept him fully as a person of dignity and worth equal to our own.

There is a mood of ecstasy in Buber's discovery of I-Thou,

[18] *I and Thou*, tr. Ronald G. Smith. (New York: Scribner's, 1958), p. 3.
[19] *Ibid.*, p. 4.
[20] *Ibid.*, p. 8.
[21] *Ibid.*, p. 11.
[22] *Ibid.*, pp. 14-16.

41

like Teilhard's *Hymn of the Universe*.[23] Does this indicate a lack of realism in their high and idealistic evaluation of man and the universe? Let us examine the evidence in their published writings. Teilhard was a man of science who patiently gathered his evidence in the dust and rock of earth. Buber as a philosopher was no mystic, he declared, because he was "enormously concerned with just this world, this painful and precious fullness of all that I see, hear, taste. I cannot wish away any part of reality. I can only wish that I might heighten this reality." [24]

Buber suffered the anguish of Nazi persecution, yet he could return to Frankfurt in 1953 to accept the Peace Prize from the German Book Trade, and respond:

I believe, despite all, that the peoples in this hour can enter into dialogue, into a genuine dialogue with one another. In a genuine dialogue each of the partners, even when he stands in opposition to the other, heeds, affirms, and confirms his opponent as an existing other.[25]

He shows that fighting begins where speech has ceased. War conquers speech, when persons are unable to speak because they no longer trust each other.

The crisis of man is a crisis of trust. And the crisis of speech, as of war and peace, is the outcome of this loss of trust. The inability to speak with each other is not only an acute symptom of our pathology, but the most urgent demand upon us.[26]

In the explosive conflict now mounting in the Near East, with passionate enmities between the Jews and the Arabs, we may well listen to the realism of Martin Buber as he dwelt in the midst of them. Speaking on hope for this hour, he says:

[23] (New York: Harper, 1965.)
[24] *Pointing the Way*, ed. and tr. Maurice S. Friedman (New York: Harper, 1957), p. 28. This essay appeared in 1914 at the beginning of World War I.
[25] *Ibid.*, p. 238.
[26] *Ibid.*, pp. 236-38.

It is necessary to overcome massive mistrust in others, and also that in ourselves . . . the universal mistrust of our age.[27]

All great civilization has been in a certain measure a Civilization of the Dialogue, . . . genuine intercourse with one another. . . . What one calls the creative spirit of men has never been anything other than the address . . . of those called to speak to those really able and prepared to hear.[28]

This does not mean blind trust or turning back to uncritical acceptance of whatever statements are made. Buber is not asking for a vague idealism, but "a more comprehending, more penetrating realism." Our aim is not to unmask or see through other persons, but to perceive more clearly the open and hidden aspects of persons in relation to each other. We need to see the other person in his manifoldness and wholeness, in his true character without prejudice, to accept and confirm him even as I need to be confirmed by him.

Only in this way can we hope to have genuine dialogue between the two camps into which mankind is split. From each viewpoint we must turn understandingly to the true needs of other peoples, without exaggerating or minimizing them. When out of the mounting antagonisms we come to see the real conflicts between genuine needs, we can begin to negotiate settlements. We must listen to each other and speak in unreserved honesty, not empty phrases, but open and courageous words without which no healing can take place.[29]

3. *Man is a creative being.* There is a mood of impatience with words, and a restless distrust of dialogue. Words are used to deceive, to control and manipulate, as we know in false propaganda and the "big sell." Negotiations in Panmunjom or Paris may not resolve the conflict or bring enduring peace. But what Buber means by genuine dialogue arising from mutual trust is a desire to listen and understand the need of the other. It is not a diatribe to hurl accusations and win a victory in the war of words by demolishing the opponent. This is not dia-

[27] *Ibid.*, p. 222.
[28] *Ibid.*, p. 224.
[29] *Ibid.*, pp. 226-28.

logue, but a "duologue," where each side delivers a monologue, unwilling to listen to the other.[30]

If man is a creative being, he will need to act. The entire history of man shows that he is an actor. He invents tools with which to make things and joins with others to create the amazing resources of a technological civilization. He forms words to create languages and communicates with other persons in a community of values exchanged and shared. He may act for or against other persons, but the range and power of his single person is strictly limited. The expanding greatness of human creativity is developed by interacting with other persons, who give and receive in mutual learning, and who sustain each other by the interchanging transactions of community life.

Paul Tillich (1886-1965) shows how human life is loaded with ambiguities by reason of the contradictions inherent in our very nature. We bear the eternal form of the human essence, yet we struggle within the finite conditions of our human existence. Life includes its own negation in the fact of death which no life can escape. While the many dimensions of this life unite in the human being, yet they are diverse potencies that may be actualized in conflicting desires and outcomes.[31]

He affirms the creativity of life, but at the same time he is aware of its destructiveness. Life is self-creative not in the original sense in which life is given by the ultimate Creator. But it is self-creative in the dynamics of growth, which is characteristic of all dimensions of life. But this growth always creates form, whether we refer to a human body, a building, a poem, or a culture. "Every new form is made possible only by breaking through the limits of an old form. In other words, there is a moment of 'chaos' between the old and the new form, a moment of no-longer-form and not-yet form." [32]

[30] See Abraham Kaplan, "The Art of Not Listening," *Time*, January 24, 1969, p. 53.

[31] Tillich, *Systematic Theology*, III (Chicago: University of Chicago Press, 1963), 11.

[32] *Ibid.*, p. 50.

This chaotic moment of transition from the old to the new form is a threat to the continuity of life. "At this crisis life may fall back to its starting point and resist creation, or it may destroy itself in the attempt to reach a new form." [33] This we find in the crisis of birth, or the creation of a new social movement, or experiments with a new artistic style. Chaotic elements are noted in the creation story of the Old Testament, indicating how chaos and creation belong to each other. The same motif appears in the struggle of monotheism against the encircling cultures with their loyalties to other gods.

A careful study of life reveals the counterforces of growth and decay going forward together in every cell of the organism. The conditions of life are the very same as the conditions of death, linked together in the ongoing process which unites decay and renewal. "Death is present in every life process from its beginning to its end." [34] This ambiguity of creation and destruction appears also in the relations to other life, where life gives birth and nourishes life, while at the same time life preys upon other life. The life-and-death struggle goes on continually, seeking a balance which is forever threatened and renewed. Yet life lives through other life by labor and propagation, by social exchange and mutual support.

The basic function of culture is to sustain, keep alive, and foster growth. The creative functions of culture we find in *theoria* and *praxis*.[35] Language grasps the encountered reality and communicates it by myth and symbol into the religious, the poetic, and the scientific theory. This liberates us from bondage to the here and now through universal concepts and images. Theory is the act of looking at the world to make of it a meaningful whole. Practice is the whole interaction of persons who as members of social groups call each other forth into creative endeavors. Labor and technology, distribution of goods and privileges may transform society according to justice. Or

[33] *Ibid.*, p. 51.
[34] *Ibid.*, p. 53.
[35] *Ibid.*, p. 62.

practical interactions may separate, exploit, deprive, and destroy the values and privileges of others.

Man's potential creativity may be enhanced or reduced by his perception of the meaning of life. The ultimate question is not what we ask of life, but what does life ask of us.[36] The task of theology, as Tillich says, is to find the ultimate meaning of life. Out of the ambiguities of our human existence we seek the meaning of life in eternal perspective. Religious faith is ultimate concern, wrestling with the doubts and uncertainties that arise in the dilemmas of our existence.

4. *Man is a self-transcending being.* The human animal, so far as we know, is the only creature who talks to himself. Other animals cry out and give signals to the mate and the young. But man talks to himself in a unique sense of dialogue. He is continually planning his future and reviewing his past. He is not wholly immersed and absorbed in the action of the moment. For he observes his action and approves or disapproves of himself for what he is doing.

Reinhold Niebuhr (1892-1971) sees this self-transcending ability as the most unique characteristic of man.[37] This constant internal dialogue is quite different from the external dialogues with other persons. Within the privacy of his inner life, each person is seeking to know who he is, and how to shape the course of his life with hope or despair, with courage and perspective, or fear and impulsive outburst.

The Bible notes this unusual capacity of man by saying that God made him in his own image and likeness. The Greek view, as developed by Plato and Aristotle, was that this divine capacity in man was his reason enabling him to make conceptual images, to comprehend the universal, and think by tracing causes in logical analysis to bring these sequences into a coherent synoptic view of all parts seen together in wholeness.

But there is more than reason in man's unique capacity of

[36] See Viktor Frankl, *Man's Search for Meaning* (Boston: Beacon Press, 1959, 1962), p. 111.

[37] Niebuhr, *The Self and the Dramas of History* (New York: Scribner's, 1955), p. 6.

freedom to enter into dialogue. Freud, in *The Ego and the Id*, saw this dialogue as a dynamic conflict of unconscious urges lusting for pleasure (id), yet repressed by the conscience representing the moral authority of parents and society (superego). In the midst of these counterforces he saw the executive self (ego) adjusting these pressures to the reality principle, and coordinating the power of the lusting id with the moral restraint of the superego. Thus a person may try to meet the expectations of others without giving up his own desires, though not to the entire satisfaction of either.

The self in Niebuhr's theology is not confined to the ego, but is actually participating in all three of these functions: impulsive desire, moral censoring, and executive adjusting to reality. The self as conscience transcends the self as primitive desire, while the self as executive ego is transcending both of these components even while participating in their functions. What Freud calls sublimation of the primitive lust (libido) is clearly a self-transcending growth toward the goal of the ego-ideal.

The transcendent character of the human self is an empirical fact observable to every person from his own inner dialogue, even though he may not use these terms to describe his self-observing activity. Niebuhr finds this a more significant testimony of the self's freedom over nature than his reason alone. For it is well known in the awareness of a self-conscious being that he is both subject and object at once, the observer and the observed. Out of this double vision the self is continually transcending himself in the complexities of his looking inward and outward, and before and after, to remember the past and project hopeful or despairing expectations into the future. At the same time he is judging himself, to pity or glory in his failures and successes, to form self-images and decide how to present himself in response to other persons and events.

But the inner dialogue is not the whole story. The Hebraic story in the Bible gives a fuller account of the uniqueness of man than the Hellenic description of reason. The larger revelation of the uniqueness of man finds him engaging in three continuing dialogues. He is in dialogue with himself, with his neighbors, and with God.

The dialogue with our neighbors is as essential to the nature of personhood as the inner dialogue within the self. Not only are we interdependent with our neighbors for sustenance and security which enables us to survive, but we are equally interdependent with them for the image one has of himself. It is only through the interchange of seeing and being seen, of address and response, of knowing others and being known by them, that we come to know who we are. Not only do we learn a language of words by responding to each other, but we learn a language of relationships, in which I perceive myself in the eyes of others, to be identified by name and called forth into social being as a member of a community, where I belong and count as a person.

The third dialogue of the self is with God. Here we are likely to find a disagreement, perhaps a boundary dispute, with those who are steeped in the Hellenic or scientific tradition of naturalism. For this assertion of dialogue with God takes us beyond the limits of objective scientific verification. We are not parted from empirical observation as we listen to the report of personal experience; yet there are those who believe we cannot establish a scientific proof for God. In this study it is not our purpose to construct proofs of God. For to treat God as one object out there, existing among other objects, is to reduce God from Ultimate Being to a finite thing among other things.

Let us rather begin with a more modest claim, that the self imagines this significant experience to be an encounter with the divine. This is not to say we deny God as Ultimate Being. Nor are we in a position to claim at this moment that we comprehend the true and infinite nature of Ultimate Being. Yet we can assert a personal experience, which is also open to others who sense such encounters, that we find ourselves responding to that which has ultimate meaning to us. From this position we can agree with Niebuhr that what distinguishes man nobly and dramatically from other animals is his yearning for the

48

ultimate. "For if we omit this characteristic we have failed to define the total anatomy of human selfhood." [38]

The tendency to identify the self with the rational mind is erroneous; and this error "obscures the freedom of the self over its rational faculties." [39] The religious inclination of men arises from this freedom to discern a mystery and meaning beyond the tight limits of reason. The task of penetrating the ultimate mystery may raise the finite to absolute value, as in idolatry and Marxism. Or it may forsake the finite as worthless trash, as in mysticism.

More discerning than either the Marxism of modern communism or the mysticism of Eastern religions is the biblical faith of Judaism and Christianity. The thesis of the biblical faith is that the self is in dialogue with a God who must be defined as a "person" because he embodies both the structures of being and a transcendent freedom.

The Biblical thesis requires a more explicit act of faith because it leaps the gap of discontinuity between man and God and because it dares to give a specific meaning to the divine, which is relevant to the partial and fragmentary meanings of history. It both fulfills and corrects these meanings, loyalties and values, and therefore has a more valid attitude toward the self's historic existence which the various rational systems affirm too simply and the mystic thesis annuls too absolutely. . . . It gives a key to the seeming mystery of our whole cultural history.[40]

Instead of reducing man to a machine, we now witness a revolution to elevate him to a person of surprising greatness in his potentiality for creativity, beyond our brightest dreams of the future. Lewis Mumford sums up his intensive study of technics by appraising the whole technical network of power, speed, mass production, automation, instant communication, and remote control. He shows the monumental miscarriages of this power complex: pollution, waste, mass destruction, and wholesale megadeaths in "peace" and war. He denies that

[38] *The Self and the Dramas of History*, p. 5.
[39] *Ibid.*, p. 61.
[40] *Ibid.*, p. 71.

man's advance from animalhood rested solely on his propensity for tool-making, in defiance of the dogma that scientific discovery and invention are the primary goal of human existence. He sees life itself as the primary phenomenon and creativity, rather than the conquest of nature, as the ultimate criterion of man's success. And he concludes:

As long as man's life prospers there is no limit to its possibilities, no terminus to its creativity; for it is part of the essential nature of man to transcend the limits of his own biological nature, and to be ready if necessary to die in order to make such transcendence possible.[41]

Just as the scientists feel that they are called upon to explode the myths spun out of the fantasies of people who develop religions based upon such fantasies, so we as theologians are called upon to attack the reductionistic myths created by the scientists. In fact, the scientist becomes the theologian when he raises serious ultimate questions about his own deductions, and the theologian becomes the scientist when he seeks to test and verify what he believes to be true. Whenever the social scientist presumes to make a statement about what man *is* from an analysis of what he *does* (descriptive studies of behavior), he invites and should receive searching questions from the theologian. When the theologian makes pronouncements about the nature of man, he will do well to consider whether or not he is aware of the actual behavior of particular men, and what implications that behavior has for the image a man has of himself. Thus a creative dialogue should be maintained. More than that, however, social scientists and theologians should be aware of how they have been shaped by a technological society. Both should be alerted especially to the need for a deeper debate at the level of the world view out of which they raise their questions. Should that not be questioned in and of itself?

[41] *The Myth of the Machine: The Pentagon of Power* (New York: Harcourt Brace Jovanovich, 1970), p. 434.

III

Automatons or Organisms?

Changing perspectives upon the person are occurring in response to the basic question of whether people are to be perceived as mechanisms or as self-transcendıng creatures. The former view arises from our excited belief that we can truly master our environment. The fact that a few may be able to gain control of powerful technical means for dominating many others is often dismissed lightly as "that's the way the cookie crumbles," or "that's the way the old ball game is played." A subtle derision of those who are too weak to resist, implying, their "softness," stupidity, or naïveté, goes along with the attitude. The advantages with which these few begin, enabling them to pull the strings of technical manipulation and thus wrest control, are ignored or assumed by them to be of little consequence. They see no reason for fearing power because they already have it, and it feeds on itself. They then charm the victims into accepting their own servitude as the blessed fruits of a technological culture. As long as their personalities are marketable (Erich Fromm), they are useful.[1]

Forceful criticisms of a behavioral psychology spawned out of the predominating world view may be seen in such recent writings as Arthur Koestler's *The Ghost in the Machine*,[2] or Ludwig Von Bertalanffy's *Robots, Men and Machines*.[3] These

[1] See Fromm, *Man for Himself: An Inquiry into the Psychology of Ethics* (New York: Holt, Rinehart and Winston, 1947), pp. 67-82.
[2] (New York: Macmillan, 1967).
[3] (New York: Braziller, 1967).

51

works demonstrate the growing concern to get at the meaning of personal spirit and to release its potential from the pernicious grip of an automated culture.

Von Bertalanffy notes that although robotistic concepts are widely denounced, they actually remain dominant in studies of man's behavior. He regards the leading concepts of man in contemporary thought as *the stimulus-response scheme, environmentalism, the equilibrium principle,* and *the principle of economy.*[4] He identifies one example of the first, or so-called S-R scheme, as "operant conditioning by reinforcement" as set forth especially by B. F. Skinner.[5] The second he also associates with behaviorism as the concept has developed from the early ideas of John Watson. The third, the principle of stability and homeostatic equilibrium, follows the thought of Sigmund Freud. The fourth concept, the principle of economy or utilitarianism, has not been associated with any particular school but has pervaded all of them to a greater or lesser degree.

These principles, or variations of them, are seen as the underlying assumptions of the most influential systems of thought regarding man and his behavior. We will cite a few of these as examples of the cultural milieu in which we find ourselves and to which we must address ourselves. We are witnessing to an expanding consciousness which values what is being perceived in essence, rather than largely as an object to be manipulated. What are we seeing when we look at someone or something? What is really there?

The inferences we draw from these studies are that reductionist theories of the person tend to "de-spiritize" man. They interpret him largely in mechanistic terms. He becomes like a robot who is hardly aware of his feelings, much less capable of acting on them. He is cut off from his real possibilities. He hardly knows his nonintellective self. He yearns to be able to feel something if only for the moment, but he seems to resign himself to cafeteria modes of experiencing—a taste here and a

[4] *General System Theory* (New York: Braziller, 1968).
[5] *Walden II* (New York: Macmillan 1948).

taste there, a week-end, or "some enchanted evening." What will give him integrity and wholeness?

We agree with Roszak when he interprets the current countercultural revolution as characterized by "*consciousness consciousness.*" [6] It is as though while going through the motions of what we are now doing, we suddenly become very conscious of ourselves and our actions from the perspective of a consciousness of "much more." That is, we become aware that our technological rituals may still our anxieties much like a tranquilizer which dulls our senses and reduces our awareness. We may feel more secure, but less alive.

1. Expanding Personal Consciousness

Most of our waking life we are surrounded by various persons whom we take for granted just because they are there. But actually we have quite an external and superficial view of them. We note how they appear to a fleeting glance and form vague impressions that may be far from the fact and largely false to the true nature of each unique person. We probably bring a narrow mind-set to frame each person, and hold it rigidly as a final opinion which excludes us from true understanding.

This mind-set is a product of all the experiences we have lived through from the first hour of birth. With the changing scenes and kaleidoscope of contrasting impressions that are impinging upon us, our view of life might well be confusing. Lest we be overwhelmed by such confusion, we defend ourselves by closure. That is, we close eyes and ears when we go to sleep and shut out all these annoying stimuli, so we can have a night's rest. And in daily life we close out many stimuli to pay attention to the one central point on which we focus. Of course we miss many exciting events this way, yet we are able to control the flow of experience by closure.

The mind-set is also a product of the culture in which we live, which places great emphasis upon the usefulness of per-

° *The Making of a Counter-Culture*, p. 62.

sons. We may tend not to be interested in persons whose usefulness to us may not be readily apparent. To be interested in them for themselves alone, as persons, may not occur to us.

A mind-set is premature closure. Seizing upon a simple proverb, or a familiar principle of common sense, we organize our belief system around these hasty conclusions and feel safe behind our defenses. Taking the proverb "Good fences make good neighbors," we build walls to shut out all but our meager supply of enclosed possessions. If we close ourselves away from the unknown and hold to the principle "Never speak to strangers," we are cut off from new interpersonal relations. To be safe we constrict our behavior. We close our mind to new ideas and to other persons who are unique in their vivid differences, if we are unwilling to risk the surprise of the unknown.

Yet the lure of the unknown is irresistibly calling the open mind to venture forth into ever new discovery. Those who respond may become scientists, explorers, artists, theologians, or engage in other far-reaching pursuits. They may become friendly and loving persons who devote themselves to the deeper knowing of other persons. Open-mindedness is a cardinal principle of these seers, as they devote themselves to exploring the unknown areas and potentialities of life in our universe. From the beginning of human history, curious minds have wondered, gathered and systematized data, to comprehend the nature of the world and all forms of life which live therein.

Gestalt psychologists focus upon the whole pattern of our seeing. At the center of the field of vision we focus sharply upon a figure. But at the same time we are aware of the background from which the figure stands out. In reading this page I focus upon the words of a line in relation to the lines before and after on the whole page. This page stands out from my perception of the book, which is on the desk, which stands against the wall, the windows, and drapes. As I read I am dimly aware of the chair supporting me, and the floor on which my feet rest. Farther out in the field of vision is the floor lamp and the room around me. So each person stands forth to me from a background of a whole context of relationships.

To perceive clearly we need a constantly changing focus. The person we meet is unique so we focus our vision upon the details of his nature to know who he is. Beneath the external appearance we search for the inner character, the motives and intentions of his behavior. And yet he reminds us of other persons we have known, and we find he does not stand alone but interacting with the persons around him. To know him more completely we come to see what other persons mean to him, and how he responds and relates to the persons and groups with whom he participates in the ongoing course of his life.

To be open-minded is to be ready to change our focus from the smallest detail to the greatest perspective. Otherwise a rigid mind-set will limit or freeze our perception in the narrow confine of a rigid viewpoint or fearful obsession. A bifocal lens is useful but quite limited in scope. What we need for adequate perception is the multifocal lens of a perfect camera, which we adjust for close-up detail or whatever distance we want to bring into sharper clarity, until we reach the horizon of enlarging perspective.

2. Stimulus and Response

This morning we met in a church for worship. Walking along the corridor we recognized persons coming out of the earlier service, parents bringing their children to the nursery, displays from Grades I, II, and III on the wall and table, books at the library counter, and a statue of a bearded Moses standing in anger about to hurl the tablets of law. Meeting our friends in the foyer, we moved up the aisle following an usher, who handed us the church bulletin as we were seated. How do we respond to these stimuli?

We have an interest in this church that led us to come with both memory and anticipation. As I lifted my eyes to the Gothic arches and stained glass, the eternal flame and the cross, I felt an elevation of spirit. For this was a spiritual home to me, and a sense of gratitude welled up within me to the Creator of life and the congregation of the faithful who formed and continue this community of aspiration and service. Looking around to see who was here, I recognized some and wondered about others. The organist was playing Bach chorales, and I settled into a quiet mood of worship with nostalgic expectation.

Then we rose to sing with marching choirs the processional hymn, and I felt a stirring unity in voicing our Christian faith with generations of persons known and unknown who have come before and will declare this faith after we are gone. Through moments of silence and prayer we confessed what we are and what we contribute to the unrest of the world through indifference, discrimination against people of a different race, reliance on weapons of terror, and preoccupation with material standards. We asked for the freedom and energy of a forgiven people, that those in bondage may be set free. The choir responded: "Ye are now sorrowful; howbeit ye shall again behold me, and your heart shall be joyful, and your joy no man taketh from you" (John 16:22).

During the sermon the minister was unfolding the story of the prodigal son, who came to himself saying, "I will arise and go to my father." He was pointing out that we all leave home to go our separate ways. Some may lose their way and others are estranged, while everyone misses in some way the greatness which is his heritage and highest potential. Then came a startling sentence I will never forget.

"Life is what we are alive to!" From here on I followed this idea which became a luminous meteor beckoning me to the course of its destiny. I was caught by its brilliance and could not turn back or blot out the vision. Is this not what distinguishes a living tree from a rock, and human life from other animal life? A growing tree is alive to the nourishing chemicals of the earth and the atmosphere. The hawk is alive to the prey on which it feeds. The newborn baby is alive to the mother's breast, the warm crib and the tender, loving care.

Yet as the human infant grows, he becomes more alive to an ever larger range of stimuli. His life is enriched and fulfilled according to the measure of his responsiveness. His entire organism is sensitive increasingly to whatever calls forth his attentive response. He never stops learning, but continues to respond in growing patterns of association to enlarging clusters of stimuli.

Many psychologists since Ivan Pavlov (1849-1936) have been showing how all learning is the product of stimulus and response. Pavlov's classic experiment was to present food as a stimulus to a laboratory dog and measure the secretion of the salivary gland as the response. A bell was sounded whenever food was presented, until the association was established. Then the bell sounded without the food, and the dog responded to the bell as he had to the food. The second stimulus produced saliva as efficiently as the first one. This training is known as *conditioning*. It can be employed to establish paths of learning with increasing complexity in the behavior of living organisms.

As we follow the course of human learning the possibilities are virtually infinite. At any rate no limits placed upon human learning have ever proved to be firm or final. For in the history of science and technology men are constantly crossing boundaries and breaking through barriers to new discoveries. Insoluable problems are solved, and the impossible becomes possible in the outreach of the human mind. Persons are continually enlarging the dimensions of their life in becoming alive to new and greater potentialities.

Yet there are restrictions weighing heavily upon our human learning. The traditions and prejudices of the past prevent and retard our freedom to move into the potential future. We are loaded with archaic and outdated presuppositions which bind our minds to the limited and distorted concepts of traditional and narrow viewpoints. Scientists may fall prey to oversimplified formulas akin to the ancient dogmas of a static religious creed. The so-called law of parsimony is a binding constriction that aims to reduce all complexities to the simplest terms. Though why an economy of scarcity and deprivation is better than an economy of abundance does not yield to scientific proof.

The reduction of all human learning to the simplified mechanism of stimulus-response conditioning is a case in point. To the laboratory experimenter seeking a neat design to fit his mechanical apparatus, the S-R learning theory is a handy gadget. Taking a bold leap of faith, he may seize the oversimplified formula as his idol, and devote his life to "proving" by many repetitions and replications that you can reduce all human behavior to the familiar S-R theory.

This reduction of human behavior to a simple S-R mechanism is calling forth a vigorous protest from other psychologists. The debate is breaking forth in the reviews and replies that contend for a larger view of what we are alive to. Dismay is expressed at the "constrained and oversimplified presentation of significant problems" in S-R theory. Arthur Staats in *Learning, Language, and Cognition*[7] declares that an adequate theory of human learning must "abstract, interrelate, and elaborate the heavyweight principles" to cope with complex environmental and behavioral events. Yet he seeks to reduce all this to simplistic S-R. He assumes his "laws" are facts beyond dispute. But his reviewer concludes: "The reader learns much more about how some hypothetical S-R mechanisms might account for selected, oversimplified phenomena than he does about the phenomena themselves, or other potentially fruitful approaches to these phenomena." [8]

In our worship in the Gothic church, we have many complex stimuli and many complex responses. If we reduce the meaning of worship to a simple S-R mechanism, we may cut away the far-reaching overtones of ultimate concern for our human destiny on this planet, and see only the animal behavior that is causally determined by a stimulus conditioned by mechanical repetition. But is this the true meaning of our experience?

[7] (New York: Holt, Rinehart and Winston, 1968).
[8] Sam Glucksberg, "A Self-Made Straw Man," *Contemporary Psychology*, XIII (December, 1968), 624-25.

3. The Experience of Relations

Another psychologist has recently undertaken to reformulate the question of learning. Solomon Asch finds the stimulus-response theory of learning restrictive and misleading by reducing complex data to simple elements.[9] Actually the most familiar and pervasive family of facts is the experience of relations. Wherever we turn we experience many kinds of relations, which form the bridges between one psychological event and another. We observe that each event is between other events in time, and every object stands with other forms of space, while every person moves from here to there among other persons. What we perceive most is not separate items, for every thing is seen in a context, and every person is found in the midst of his network of relationships.

It would be naïve to assume that objects coexist out there in separation from each other and the person observing them. To perceive relations is an act of bringing together many data into coherent unity, as we shall see more clearly in taking a new look at how we perceive. The S-R theorists are seeing relations in the one association of contiguity. And Pavlov's dog is perceiving the relation of food and bell, until he comes to expect food whenever the bell sounds. If the food never comes again, he will eventually perceive the bell is not related to food, and will no longer respond with saliva when the bell sounds.

But when psychologists hold that elements are the real things, they overlook the significance of relations, as if they were transient and must be broken up into discrete data to get at the basic unity of learning. To correct this fallacy of the isolated unit, we must recognize that facts are interdependent and have meaning only as we perceive their relationships. A relation cannot be resolved into a fact about one term plus a fact about another term. "To experience a relation is to apprehend the terms simultaneously and also the mode of transition between them." [10]

[9] Asch, "A Reformulation of the Problem of Associations," *American Psychologist*, XXIV (February, 1969), 92-102.
[10] *Ibid.*, p. 94.

By a series of experiments with geometric figures and nonsense syllables, Dr. Asch studies memory recall and points to recognition as the essential step in recalling a memory trace. No recall is possible, and new learning is required, unless the subject recognizes the relationship. Recognition is a personal act of interrelating previous experience with present interest. The external association of events is not able to produce recall. Nor can we recall by neural paths caused by conditioning or repetition, until we recognize the relation in the experience of this present moment. Evidently the shape of our perception is not given to us by external or prior associations upon a passive mind. But rather we can recall only by actively reaching out to recognize the relationship, drawing the memory of the past into a vivid reliving of its meaning in the present. The recognition is a present discovery of new meaning in the previous events recorded as memory.

These relations experienced in the past return to us in the act of recognition and recall. We project our expectations into the future by relating what we have known to what we are hoping we can foresee and create, if we are responsible to the ongoing tasks and goals that pull us forward. And we reach out to other persons to see how we can relate to them. Observing another person holds him at a distance. Empathy draws us nearer to the other person by entering into his experience to feel what life means to him in his situation. Prejudice holds us against the other person by judging him unfavorably and resisting what he is, or appears to be, in our hostile eyes. In each of these moving experiences we seek to explore and perceive our relations to other persons.

4. The Person: Shaped or Shaping

Is the person largely determined by outside influences? Does he begin life as a blob of protoplasm which can be shaped into almost any desirable end? Do changes in social structures automatically produce changes in him? Undoubtedly the way we have phrased these questions invites a negative reply. Yet we feel we are being true to assumptions of those who feel that manipulation of the environment can produce creative individuals.

One way of putting the presupposition of the environmentalists is: "The secret of health and happiness lies in successful adjustment to the ever-changing conditions on this globe; the penalties for failure in this great process of adaptation are disease and unhappiness." [11] The truth in this statement is well known to people who have foolishly tried to defy basic facts of life, such as building fancy towering geometric edifices over faults in the earth's crust. The high probability of earthquake damage is a fact of life. Yet to argue insistently for adaptive principles or to manipulate the environment is to play down creativity, if not to negate it altogether.

The person shapes himself as he becomes self-actualizing, which means he is realizing his potentialities. We tend to agree with Abraham Maslow, who has said:

If one is preoccupied with the insane, the neurotic, the psychopath, the criminal, the delinquent, the feeble-minded, one's hopes for the human species become perforce more and more modest, more and more realistic, more and more scaled down. One expects less and less from people.

Psychology has not stood up to its full height . . . or what it MIGHT be, if it could free itself from the stultifying effects of limited . . . preconceptions about human nature. [12]

Our preoccupation with pathological norms for personality has had characteristically reductionistic effects on theories of the person. Maslow has made the point that we have for too long sold human nature short. He has raised the decisive question: What are self-actualizing people like? His studies show that manipulating the environment is not the whole answer. Some people have become uniquely self-actualizing depite environmental conditions that have apparently defeated others.

[11] H. Selye, *The Stress of Life* (New York: McGraw-Hill, 1956), p. vii.
[12] *Motivation and Personality* (New York: Harper, 1954), pp. 360, 354.

He notes that their basic motives make the difference. Those who view life negatively (deficit motives) are defeated by an unfavorable environment, but those who actualize themselves positively (growth motives) tend to shape rather than be shaped by their environment.

These basic attitudes, Maslow asserts, stem from how well the basic needs of the person are being met. The basic needs are physiological—food, liquid, shelter, sex, sleep, and oxygen; safety—consistency, fairness, and a dependable routine; belongingness—love and affection; esteem—self-respect and esteem from others; self-actualization—the desire to become more than we are; knowledge—satisfaction of curiosity, to understand and to systematize, and to look for meanings; aesthetic needs—to find beauty in one's surroundings; and growth needs—wholeness, completion, justice, aliveness, etc. Maslow observed clinically that the frustration of these needs led to pathological symptomatology. Satisfaction of the basic needs produced healthy personalities. These needs are not environmental, but intensely *personal*. We can have ideal conditions of the environment, but fail to give the person the "stroking" he needs. Hence we deny him satisfaction of his basic needs, and therefore should not be surprised if he exhibits psychopathological symptoms in spite of his favorable environment.

"The various behaviorisms all seem to generate inexorably such a passive image of a helpless man, one who has . . . little to say about his . . . own fate." [13] Man is much more capable of shaping his existence in ways that reflect his sense of the divine image in him than the reductionistic behavioral scientists appear to recognize.

5. Stability vs. Viability

The principle of stability was held to be at the core of Sigmund Freud's theory of the deep motivation of the organism

[13] Maslow, *The Psychology of Science* (New York: Harper, 1966), p. 55.

to attain homeostatic equilibrium. He derived this principle from clinical observations of subjects in psychoanalysis. Maslow's critique of Freud's views show his concern to move beyond a reductionist stance. Maslow felt Freud's picture of man was clearly unsuitable, leaving out as it did, his aspirations, his realizable hopes, his Godlike qualities. "Freud supplied to us the sick half of psychology and we must now fill it out with the healthy half." [14]

Following Maslow's lead, we advocate moving from the principle of stability to what we call the principle of viability, by which we mean the zest for living. This goes beyond the avoidance or reduction of tensions. In fact tensions may be heightened in the struggle for fulfilling goals. Zest for living includes the appropriation of values. His concern for morals and purposes enhances the living capacity and enjoyment of the truly self-actualizing person. Viability, then, is more expansionist, while stability is reductionist in its total effect upon the personality. We are using the term "viability" to convey this broader meaning. "Living life to the full" seems to be too much of a slogan to interpret the real meaning of the word, but the phrase gets at what we intend to affirm.

We are not rejecting behaviorism *in toto*. We do not regard behaviorists as bogeymen. We find the techniques of behaviorists helpful and useful. However, when they begin to spin out theories predicated upon reductionist presuppositions, we find them too narrow and constricting.

We have intended in this chapter to refer briefly to principles which have been derived from reductionistic views of man. These principles tend to support interpretations, the logical consequences of which are to regard people as kinds of automatons. They may function well as parts of the system, but they have been desensitized. Even the industries, which in some measure contribute to the dehumanization process, are suffi-

[14] Maslow, *Toward a Psychology of Being* (New York: Van Nostrand, 1962), p. 5.

IV

Tribunes of the Personal

In ancient Rome tribunes were the protectors of the plebians of the city. In a real sense they were spokesmen of the people. For that reason they became known as "champions of the people." We feel that prophetic voices both within and outside the church are being raised in behalf of persons in our society. We regard these voices as belonging to modern "champions of the personal." In this chapter we will refer to several whose impact has been widely felt. In later chapters we will introduce others quite briefly, but will not deal with them as systematically as we do here.

As alternatives to depersonalizing reductionist theories, we affirm the views of Viktor Frankl, Eric Berne, Frederick Perls and the Gestaltists, and the contributions of those who are regarded by Abraham Maslow as "The Third Force"—Maslow, Carl Rogers, Kurt Goldstein, Gordon Allport. We are interested less in giving a smorgasbord of personality theories and more in recognizing those whom we regard as contributing in some measure to the "revolution of the personal." We conclude this chapter with our own views of the person and his tremendous possibilities for self-actualization and creativity. We speak of the critical dimensions of his relationships, through which personal growth is activated.

1. Meaning and Intuition

Viktor Frankl is a leading psychiatrist of Vienna who has profound concern for the meaning of life. He sees the loss of meaning as the cause of emptiness and despair among 80 percent of the people he has studied in Europe and America. Without meaning life is worthless and intolerable; many attempt suicide or throw themselves into a futile pursuit of success or pleasure that only deepens the hopelessness of their existential vacuum.

When the Nazi forces moved into Austria, they brought ruthless pressure and death upon millions of Jews whom they attacked as aliens. What attitude, Frankl asked, could give meaning to life under such cruel and fanatical persecution as this? He was offered an immigration visa by the American Consulate in Vienna. This seemed at first to be the open door to freedom and a new life. Should he accept?

My old parents expected me to leave Austria as soon as the visa was given. However, at the last moment I hesitated: The question of whether I should leave my parents beset me. I knew that any day they could be taken to a concentration camp. Shouldn't I stay with them? While pondering this question I found that this was the type of dilemma which made one wish for a hint from Heaven. It was then I noticed a piece of marble lying on a table at home. When I asked my father about it, he explained that he had found it on the site where the National Socialists had burned down the largest Viennese synagogue. My father had taken this marble piece home because it was a part of the tablets which contained the Ten Commandments. The piece showed one engraved and gilded Hebrew letter. My father explained that this letter was an abbreviation for only one of the Commandments. Eagerly I asked, "Which one is it?" The answer was: "Honor thy father and thy mother: that thy days shall be long upon the land." So I stayed with my father and mother upon the land and decided to let the American visa lapse.[1]

This was an intuitive perception of himself in relation to his parents. He suddenly knew what he was called to do, and whatever the danger he accepted his responsibility to remain with his parents to help them in any way possible. What was the controlling stimulus to call forth this decision? The piece of marble was not the only stimulus, or even the words of his

[1] *Psychotherapy and Existentialism: Selected Papers on Logotherapy* (New York: Washington Square Press, 1967), p. 34. Reprinted by permission of Simon & Schuster.

father. They were but signals evoking the great challenge of the biblical heritage. There was the sense of ultimate meaning in life and death, and of a destiny beyond his own comfort and safety. His basic attitude of reverence for life, and faithfulness to heaven was to him a steady ongoing vocation which he would not renounce for any prosperity or pleasure that could lure him to turn aside from what he saw to be his truest decision.

Commenting upon this crucial moment of intuition, he believes that seeing the piece of marble as a hint from heaven reveals the fact "that long before, in the depth of my heart, I had decided to stay. I only projected this decision into the appearance of the marble piece." [2] Otherwise he might have seen the marble as a totally different stimulus, nothing but $CaCo_3$. Out of the data of this moment he chose the meaning by which to guide the course of his life. He might have chosen another course, and from that time on he would have followed a very different road. As he comments further on this decision:

Man cannot avoid decisions. Reality inescapably forces man to decide. Man makes decisions in every moment, even unwittingly and against his will. Through these decisions man decides upon himself. Continually and incessantly he shapes and reshapes himself. . . . Man is not a thing among others—things determine each other—but man is ultimately self-determining. What he becomes —within the limits of endowment and environment—he has made himself. [3]

When he and his family were seized by the Nazi troopers and sent to concentration camps, Viktor Frankl was faced with many crucial decisions, from the moment when an officer's finger pointed him away from the gas chambers to a work camp. He was stripped not only of his clothing and eyeglasses, but his family, his medical practice, his social position, and the manuscript of the book he was intending to publish. A great deal of meaning was lost in such ruthless stripping and inhuman treatment. Would it be better to die?

[2] *Ibid.,* p. 34.
[3] *Ibid.,* p. 35.

He soon discovered that prisoners who lost interest in life died within a few days under the lash of cruelty and starvation. He talked with them in the long hours of darkness about holding some vital meaning beyond the prison camp to live for, to enable them to defy the hopeless present with a goal of larger meaning in the future—some loved one to meet or task to fulfill, plans to make and dreams to hope for eventual fulfillment. Ultimately, he said, every person is irreplaceable, and no one else can fulfill the meaning that is his personal responsibility.[4]

Love and conscience, he holds, are both intuitive capacities of self-transcendence. Love is the capacity to hold another person in the unique quality of his spirit and destiny whose place no one else can take. Conscience is the capacity to grasp the meaning of a situation in its concrete uniqueness as a challenge to personal responsibility. The fulfillment of such meaning always requires deciding who I will be and to whom I will devote myself.[5]

2. Transaction and Analysis

There are various ways of perceiving a human organism. Behaviorists see man from an external viewpoint as an animal who operates in patterns of stimulus and response. Freud sees man from an internal point of view as a dynamic mechanism of action and reaction. The mental apparatus, as he perceives it, is largely unconscious energy pressing for release. The action springs from a deep fountain of primitive urges, "a seething cauldron of excitement," which he calls the *id*, lusting for pleasure and striving as hunger and sexual craving for gratification. This striving is amoral; it has no sense of right or wrong, time or place. It is the impulsive action of raw vitality arising insistently as life itself, powered by instinctual drives (*trieben*). This lusty vitality he calls *libido*.

[4] *Man's Search for Meaning: An Introduction to Logotherapy* (New York: Washington Square Press, 1963), p. 127.
[5] *The Will to Meaning: Foundations and Applications of Logotherapy* (New York: World, 1969), pp. 19, 43.

With no guiding control this primitive energy of life is dangerously destructive. Parents intervene to protect the growing child, to nourish his hunger for love and food, to guide his first steps, to curb his reckless demands, and to educate him to exercise inner control of his impulsive life. A counterforce, which Freud calls the *superego*, is formed by the example and teaching of parents and other authorities to caution, restrain, and repress these primitive energies. Action from the id below calls forth reaction from the superego above in dynamic struggles for ascendancy. This inner conflict never ceases until death brings the struggle to a conclusion, and these counterforces subside into quiescence.

Psychoanalysis is a theory by which to understand, and a therapy by which to heal, the inner conflicts and find a way of balancing these counterforces. The aim is to develop the *ego* as the moderator or executive who considers the claims of both the impulsive id and the moral superego, to find a reasonable solution to these conflicts. The conscious ego faces outward to the reality of the world around us, the needs of the community, and the expectations of other persons. The ego may become aware of the ideal person he seeks to become, and sublimate the primitive impulses to uphold and empower this ideal quest. The ego may identify with other persons and introject their qualities and virtues into his own character. The goal of psychoanalysis is therefore to strengthen the ego to cope with inner needs and outer requirements, to reconcile the conflicting forces, and decide how to conduct life according to the reality principle and the ego ideal. "Where id was, there shall ego be." [6]

Another way of perceiving man is to see him as a person engaging in transactions with other persons. For life is incomplete and unfulfilling in isolation. It is impossible to understand one person alone apart from his responses to other persons. "No man is an island," for every person is involved with other persons in the interchange of mutual interests and concerns.

[6] Sigmund Freud, *Introductory Lectures on Psychoanalysis* (New York: W. W. Norton, 1964), p. 80.

Infants deprived of handling will decline and die. Persons need to be recognized and affirmed by other persons to fulfill the meaning of human life.

A unit of social intercourse is known as a transaction. One person behaves in a certain way with the intention of drawing a response from another person. Eric Berne defines this as the transactional stimulus. The person responding gives the transactional response. "The intention of getting a response is what makes the aggregation a social one."[7] The analysis of a unit of social action is called transactional analysis.

To analyze transactions Berne begins with a study of the structure of the human personality as it is observed to function in social interaction. Changes in posture, muscle tone, facial expression, gestures, voice, vocabulary, and emotional quality are observed as persons respond to each other. Three predominating ego states appear, each forming a coherent pattern of feeling and behavior. These ego states may be identified as:

(1) those that resemble the ego state of a parent;

(2) those ego states that are autonomously directed toward appraisal of reality; and

(3) those ego states reflecting those found in a young child.

These three ego states are designated as (1) the Parent, (2) the Adult, and (3) the Child. These aspects of personality are parallel to Freud's analysis of the superego, the ego, and the id. Yet Berne declares they are not identical, as he uses these concepts to analyze social transactions. In contrast to this, Freud uses his structure to analyze the inner conflicts emerging from unconscious determinants.

When social transactions are complementary, they operate smoothly to achieve the mutual intentions. For example, a man with a fever goes to bed in the ego state of his Child, and his wife nurses him in the ego state of a Parent. They are mutually responsive to and fulfilled by each other in these roles. Communication can proceed and continue along such complementary lines.

[7] *The Structure and Dynamics of Organization and Groups* (New York: Grove Press, 1966), p. 129.

But communication is broken off when crossed transaction occurs. The husband may give an Adult-Adult stimulus by asking, "Do you know where my cuff links are?" The appropriate A-A response would be, "On the desk." So far they are participating in an Adult-Adult transaction.

If instead the wife responds, "You always blame me for everything," we have a crossed transaction in which the wife responds from the ego state of her Child. If he warms up to the argument with a petulant tone to say, "You must have put them somewhere," they are now responding Child to Child.

However, if we return to the beginning with the husband's Adult question, "Do you know where my cuff links are?" another response is possible. The wife may say, "Why don't you keep track of your own things? You're not a child anymore." She has crossed his Adult stimulus with her Parent response, and communication is tangled up. This may be shown by the following diagram: [8]

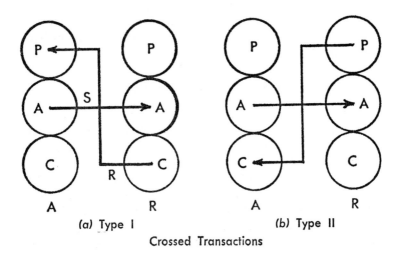

(a) Type I (b) Type II

Crossed Transactions

[8] Berne, *Games People Play*, Copyright © 1964 by Eric Berne. Reprinted by permission of Grove Press, Inc.

71

At this point the husband may respond from his angry Child, and they may indulge in a game of Uproar in which neither is going to yield or accept the reality, but contend with each other in a game for some ulterior gain to defeat the other or prove superiority over the other.

An easier outcome would be for the husband to chuckle and agree we are both Adults who can work out a simple problem with lost cuff links. Keeping his cool he may reach for another pair so they will not be late for their engagement.

Yet simple transactions are likely to be superficial and deceptive, to cover up deeper feelings and elude a confrontation with the other person. The complexity of our natures gives vitality and depth to human relations, in which we may choose who we will be in response to the other person. We may choose to play games defensively to fend others off. Or we may find the painful freedom of open communication a way to be honest and accept each other as we are.

We can use the wisdom of the Parent and the vital spontaneity of the Child to enrich the reasonable practicality of the Adult. Yet each will serve us best in balance and proportion to the other ego states, as we give the full range of our human responses to the versatile transactions we are to have with other persons.

3. Encounter and Facilitation

Carl Rogers has sought to promote the "revolution in the personal" within the framework of a scientific world view. He urges a phenomenological approach to the study of the person which allows the person himself to be a member of the research team. "Suppose we enlisted every 'subject' as an 'investigator'!" he postulates. "Instead of the wise researcher measuring changes in his subjects. suppose he enlisted them all as co-researchers." [9] Arguing that the "subject" influences the research anyway, by his temperament and feeling for the researcher, Rogers asks why it is not logical to bypass all that

[9] *Carl Rogers on Encounter Groups* (New York: Harper, 1970), p. 165.

and secure the subject's participant cooperation. Tacitly, this puts more faith in the subjective consciousness than most orthodox scientific investigators are willing to allow. Actually, therefore, Rogers is asking for a broader and more inclusive view of scientific endeavor.

Thus, although Rogers does not attack the predominating scientific world view, he asks for its modification. He believes that "intensive group experiences" represent the most rapidly spreading and potent of the social inventions of the century. Amplifying this view he says:

One element which makes this phenomenon well worth psychological study is the fact that it has grown up entirely outside the "establishment.". . . I know of few other trends which have so clearly expressed the need and desire of *people* rather than institutions.[10]

The emphasis, in Rogers' latest approach, is on basic encounter groups, which are intended to work on personal growth and development and foster interpersonal communication through experiential processes. A small unstructured group chooses its own goals and directions. Expressions of feelings and thoughts of the members flow from a safe psychological climate, and mutual trust develops. Thus the members of the group become open to their own feelings and to the communications of others. They learn from the other members of the group. They also teach them. The increased flow of feelings, ideas, and communications carries over into other groups and experiences outside of the group.

The leader's responsibility is seen as largely facilitative. As a facilitator, the leader develops a climate of safety in which freedom of expression and yielding of defenses can occur. Thus he enables other members of the group to become facilitative persons in the group.

In his discussion of facilitative persons in groups, Rogers disclaims the expert's role as leader of a group. He states his goal as that of becoming a participant, although it is clear that

[10] *Ibid.*, pp. 1-2.

he does not mean to abdicate his responsibility for leadership. However, he interprets that responsibility as being *to* the persons in that group and not *for* them. Hopefully, nondefensiveness and spontaneity will develop in the group, and each member will also be responsible *to* other members of the group.

Rogers uses the analogy of the organism to describe the group. Thus his view is consonant with the organismic world view which we see as offering a viable alternative model to the mechanistic models often presented.

4. Holism and Mystery

Frederick Perls and the Gestaltists see perceptions as patterned wholes generated by the relationship between the person and his environment. The larger view is of a continuous flow and relationship between the perceiver and what he is perceiving. To envision the environment as separate or against one is already to exhibit a psychic conditioning which tends to segment the "organism/environmental field."

Neurosis, then, is the result of the divisiveness which occurs when the person regards that which is external as alien or hostile. Such a person withdraws within himself and is diminished to a being much less than his potential. In his defensiveness he also must carefully regulate what is "out there" to keep it as nonthreatening as possible and to protect what is left of himself from the hostile environment.

The Gestaltists see the latter as a lack or loss of faith in the natural processes of the body and of the emotions. Thus the person yields authority over his body and emotions to experts who can plan and regulate everything and make him feel safe and secure. It is a costly way of resolving the ambiguities of his existence, because the price is to shatter the "organism/environment" unity.

What we have said applies also to the language of communication—the challenge to bring *what* is said and *how* it is said together into a unified whole. The honesty of the man comes through showing who he is in his speech, his feelings, and his actions. "He is of a piece" is often said of the person who presents himself in openness. Such a person is vulnerable because he is exposing himself, but in his frankness he challenges the other to meet him with equal candor.

Aggressiveness is not regarded with suspicion, but is given freedom of expression. In Gestalt therapy a person who is repressing his anger and aggressiveness is encouraged to give it vent. He is not "talked through" it; he is led to experience the pent-up feelings. He is challenged to act out his frustrations. He is not shamed for behaving like a child who kicks and screams when he is frustrated, but is allowed to express his "Child" in just those ways if he feels like it.

Although the Gestaltists predicate their views on what they regard as natural, they do not give a clear explanation of what they mean by nature. What feelings, behaviors, etc., are natural to man? May there not be as many pretensions in their views as in those they attack? Despite the important contributions they make to the revolution of the personal, they do not account for how people get fragmented and become alien to their environment in the first place. Nevertheless, they opt for spontaneity, imagination, and directness of experiencing, and thus open persons to their unfolding possibilities.

5. Concretion and Relationship

Another way of perceiving a person is through existential analysis as developed by Viktor Frankl. In each perception we begin with the life that is given to us. Just as the newborn is expelled from the womb into a larger world where he has many discoveries to explore and many lessons to learn, so are we thrown into the midst of the world and confronted with life coming to meet us. We respond to the stimulus (say the behaviorists), we act and react (says Freud), we transact a social stimulus to get a social response (says Berne). We are here in the midst of our existence (says Frankl), in the world

75

of ongoing events with other persons, seeking the meaning of life.

In our time many persons have lost the meaning of life. They are baffled and confused, frustrated and defeated, or empty in the apathy and despair of an existential vacuum. Then we need to analyze our predicament to see where we are, what is missing, how we lost our way, and how to find new meaning in life. It is not for us to ask petulantly what is the meaning of life, for we are the ones who are being asked. Each situation in life is a challenge to which each person must give the answer by answering for his own life. How will we respond to the baffling situations presented to us?

We evade the issue before us when we seek an abstract meaning of life. This is like asking what is the best move in a game of chess. There is no best move in general until we know the previous move and the formation of this concrete situation. Then whatever the specific situation is confronting us, we must respond to that as best we can to fulfill our calling. We can only respond if we are response-able; i.e., by being responsible.[11]

The meaning of life is found in the concrete task that is our challenge to meet to the best of our ability. Each person has to decide for himself how he will be responsible, whether to society or his own conscience. Yet in the midst of each concrete situation as we move from one task to another we seek an overarching purpose, a sense of larger destiny which binds all events and all our strivings into one great meaning.[12] This is what Tillich calls "ultimate concern," and which he identifies as the central meaning of any truly religious quest.

There is a quality of self-transcendence in human existence, a haunting perception or dawning vision that life is more than that which appears in the fleeting impressions of our senses. The essence of every person is that inner center of his unique spirit by which he responds to that which is greater than him-

[11] Frankl, *Man's Search for Meaning*, p. 172.
[12] *Ibid.*, p. 174.

self. This transcendent capacity to see beyond the local event, to desire beyond the moment, and respond to a more ultimate meaning is the truly human dimension of our life. We falter without a strong ideal to guide and unify our efforts. Being human is directed to someone other than myself.

This dynamic tension between self and other is noted by Rudolf Allers as "the realm of the trans-subjective," [13] in which person meets person, and the subject is fulfilled in communicating with other subjects. Frankl calls this the realm of "noödynamics" to indicate the dynamic power of the spirit (noos) which enables a person to be free and responsible to the concrete task and the person who calls him forth to participate in the ultimate meaning of his life.[14]

To recognize the transcendent nature of human existence is to keep the door open to religious meaning. To Frankl life is incomplete on a two-dimensional plane, for man is a spirit who responds to a higher dimension. The ratio between man and animal is indicative of the ratio between God and man.

If I point to something with my finger, the dog does not look in the direction in which I point, it looks at my finger and sometimes snaps at my finger. It cannot understand the semantic function of pointing to something. And what about man? Is he not, too, sometimes unable to understand the meaning of something, say the meaning of suffering, and does not he, too, quarrel with his fate and and snap at its finger?

Man is incapable of understanding the ultimate meaning of human suffering because "mere thinking cannot reveal to us the highest purpose," as Albert Einstein once said. I would say that the ultimate meaning, or as I prefer to call it, the supra-meaning is no longer a matter of thinking but rather a matter of believing. We do not catch hold of it on intellectual grounds but on existential grounds, out of our whole being, i.e., through faith.[15]

[13] "Ontoanalysis: A New Trend in Psychiatry," *Proceedings of the American Philosophical Association* (1961), p. 78; quoted by Frankl, *The Will to Meaning*, p. 50.

[14] *Man's Search for Meaning*, p. 166.

[15] *The Will to Meaning*, p. 145.

Even though we may not break through the dimensional difference between the human world and the divine world, we can reach out for ultimate meaning through faith. Such basic trust makes a profound difference to us, for we are caught in a helpless paralysis either to see or to act in the potential greatness of our human vocation unless we have faith. How can man move a limb, says Frankl, unless from the depths of his being he is imbued by trust in the ultimate meaning of his life?

To those who ask if God is dead, Frankl replies: "God is not dead but silent." [16] The ultimate being, the living God, must always be a hidden God. For he is not one among many as we finite creatures are, who beckon and call to each other. Nor is he like the bottom of the ocean to echo back our sound waves. The infinity of God is boundless as the sky. We do not see the sky, but only the cloud which is hiding the sky. Nor do we see God in the telescope, for he is greater and vaster than any star or galaxy. He is not exhausted in all the stars or lightyears of space, for he is infinitely more than these. He defies reification, for we cannot make him into a thing.

The dimensional difference between being and things, or God as infinite and man as finite, prevents our speaking of God to describe him in the anthropomorphic symbols of our little minds. Yet personification of God is justified in the experience of communion of spirit with spirit, from dimension to dimension as I and Thou. Even though we cannot speak of God, we may speak to God.[17] In such communion we have joy in his presence, to find hope in the midst of suffering and faith to give our best in the sustaining power of a greater love.

6. Perspective and Whole Response

There is much to discover about persons by analysis. The work of understanding in accurate detail could not be carried

[16] *Ibid.*, p. 154.
[17] *Ibid.*, p. 146.

on without it. The microscope and X ray reveal the intricate wonder of the inner structure of the human body. Yet to magnify the cells of each organ is not yet to see the interacting system of the whole organism. The focus of seeing has to move from the infinitesimal part to the more infinite whole in larger perspective. The distant view of man is also revealing, in the long sweep of historical time, the broad spectrum of all his relationships, and the future orientation of his goals and purposes.

When the space craft Apollo 8 leaped into its 500,000-mile orbit around the moon in December, 1968, the three astronauts were given this distant view of the earth-home of man. As their life was televised and their voices recorded in the Houston control station, they said:

I'm looking out of my center window, which is the round window, and the window is bigger than the earth right now. . . . The earth is very bright. . . . It is a beautiful, beautiful view with predominantly blue background and just huge covers of clouds. . . . It is very, very beautiful. . . .

The vast loneliness up here of the moon is awe-inspiring and it makes you realize just what you have back there on earth. . . . The sky up here is also rather forbidding, foreboding extents of blackness. . . .

And from the crew of Apollo 8, we pause with good night. . . . And God bless all of you . . . all of you on the good earth.

In a remarkable search for perspective Anne Morrow Lingberg asks, after watching the launching and return of Apollo 8, what causes the overwhelming sense of joy and awe in response to this event of man in space. What does it express? The sheer power and supremacy of the machine is not the cause of such a wave of hope and elation:

What lifts our hearts today seems to be more in the realm of the human, the psychological, and the spiritual. Our response may still be too profound to reach the surface of words. Centuries may pass before man will know the promise of Apollo 8, or can assess the true meaning of this age and the new view of man and his planet—a view as revolutionary as the one Galileo illumined with his telescope.[18]

She quotes Teilhard de Chardin: "To see, or to perish, is the condition of man." This space voyage man may see as a manifestation of his destiny, a spearhead of the forward thrust of his evolution. What comes through the eyes of the astronauts is a "new-old sense of mystery and awe" before the marvels of this solar system, and a humility before its laws. In the words of Teilhard again: "Our concept of God must be extended as the dimensions of our world are expanded." There is a renewed sense of harmony with the universe. "We have been given another image of ourselves and our place in the cosmos," which enables us to know ourselves in new perspective.

How do we comprehend the wholeness of life in larger perspective?

An abstract definition or mathematical formula will not suffice. To show the richness and complexity of the human person, we need to draw upon concrete images from art, literature, and science. These are symbols which participate in the reality they present. Words and signs are also symbolic, yet the power to convey concrete images of our existence cannot be abstracted from life. The living symbol is not cut and dried, but deeply rooted in the soil from which life grows. We must communicate the meaning of life, therefore, in the symbols that arise from our being in the world that is our home.

Metaphors are figures of speech in which words bear additional meanings beyond their literal and original sense. The metaphor is a bridge to transfer enriching meanings from the past to the future. It projects outward from one traditional meaning to another meaning enlarged by implied transition to a larger context. "The Lord is my shepherd" gathers up the literal meaning of tending sheep, and projects this toward the invisible God who cares for his people. This vivid metaphor is further enriched by Jesus: "I am the good shepherd. The good shepherd lays down his life for the sheep."

[18] Anne Morrow Lindberg, "The Heron and the Astronaut," *Life*, February 28, 1969, p. 26.

Metaphors are useful in scientific as well as religious communication. Zoologist Desmond Morris writes a book on *The Naked Ape*,[19] in which he transfers the original meaning of ape to man. With this metaphor he expounds his theory of evolution to show how man belongs to the family of 193 living species of monkeys and apes, and how he can be better understood in relation to this heritage. Though man has become so proud and erudite to hold himself a higher race, the fact remains he is an animal with old impulses that have been with him for millions of years. Morris turns the metaphor into a search for the typical behavior of man as a biological creature who may dress up and cover up his animal nature, yet is after all the naked ape.

Analogies also enrich our perception of the complex nature of our living relationships. The analogy is a vivid way of showing the resemblance in some particulars between events or beings otherwise unlike. The power of analogy is to point out the richness of a paradox by seeing that a deeper unity underlies apparent differences. At the same time we discover more lively contrasts in what at first appeared to be similar. In thus knowing the complexity of life as unity in diversity, we come to deeper understanding of human life in new perspectives.

There is always more to any situation than we see at the moment. To bring out the hidden meanings and potentialities beneath the surface, we need to recognize the significance of what is not yet revealed. This we may see more clearly by analogies, which break through the shell of the obvious to the fertile egg or seminal growth that is hidden within.

Jesus awakened the minds of his hearers by analogies which he created in the form of vivid parables.

The kingdom of heaven is like leaven which a woman took and hid in three measures of meal, til it was all leavened.

The kingdom of heaven is like a grain of mustard seed which a man took and sowed in his field; it is the smallest of all seeds, but when it has grown it is the greatest of shrubs and becomes a tree,

[19] (New York: Dell Publishing Company, 1967).

so that the birds of the air come and make nests in its branches. (Matt. 13:31-33.)

When the disciples asked Jesus why he talked to the people in parables, he said: "It is because they look but do not see, and they listen, but do not hear or understand" (Matt. 13:13). The knowledge of the secrets of the kingdom of heaven is given to those who can see and understand. For those who have some understanding will be able to perceive more fully. But without this deeper understanding, nothing will be clear, and even the little one has will be lost.

Among the psychologists who are seeking to understand human behavior through the study of animals, there is the analogy that animal behavior can reveal the nature of man. This we have already met in Pavlov, whose laboratory experiments with dogs have pioneered so many studies of learning by stimulus-response conditioning. Frankl offers the analogy of dog and man to show the limits of man in his finite dimension when he seeks God in the infinite dimension. And he employs this analogy to show the capacity to trust in God. When a dog is ill, and you bring him to a veterinarian to treat him, the dog does not understand the meaning of the pain or the purpose of the needle that hurts him. Yet looking to you in boundless trust, he quietly endures the pain which the doctor causes him.[20]

Models also enable us to perceive whole responses in perspective. Scientific theories are usually based upon some model. And our perception of man reflects the model which stands before us in our theological perspectives, as we have seen in the first chapter. Whatever system we hold in philosophy or political debate, whether individualism or absolutism, will arise from the design we take as our model. Children take parents as their models to emulate. Coming into the stage of young adulthood, they face the generation gap, and may cast off the parent mold for new ones. This is the identity crisis, which Erikson so

[20] *The Will to Meaning*, p. 145.

clearly portrays, when each person has to decide for himself who he will be.[21]

Wolfgang Köhler (1887-1967) was one of the pioneers in Gestalt psychology, which seeks to understand perception as a whole response to a situation. Each situation is a complex pattern of related lines and forms which cannot be understood as discrete parts but as a larger whole (*Gestalt*). To find the meaning of a situation we need to perceive the larger scene in the complex relationships which unify the whole into clearer perspective.

His study of laboratory chimpanzees led Köhler to conclude that *insight* is the unifying perception by which the meaning of a situation is perceived.[22] Sultan was the chimpanzee who showed the power of insight most clearly in perceiving the meaning of situations. He had learned to use a stick to reach through the bars of his cage for bananas. Then he was offered a bunch of bananas hanging from the ceiling, but too high for him to reach. He could not solve this problem without insight to perceive the whole situation in perspective. He tried the stick, which was too short. Then he fitted two sticks together, but was still unable to reach the bananas. Then he went around the corner and brought a box to stand on. When he was still unable to reach the bananas he brought another box to put on top of the first one. By seeing the situation as a whole he was then able to organize these sticks and boxes to reach his prize.

What model shall we take to portray the nature of man? The animal model is a popular scientific design for understanding man in the biological and psychological sciences. Pavlov and those who study S-R conditioning in animal learning offer the dog or rat model to reveal the nature of man. Köhler employs a chimpanzee model to show how learning develops by insight into the meaning of the whole situation.

[21] Erik Erikson, *Identity and the Life Cycle* (New York: International Universities Press, 1959).

[22] Köhler, *The Mentality of Apes* (New York: Harcourt Brace, 1926).

Yet it is perhaps more true to see that man becomes the model for the chimpanzee. In Köhler's experimental work the chimpanzees are not isolated from human beings but live in the same working colony with them. They observe how the men behave in bringing food, caring for their needs, selecting sticks and boxes to use, and organizing situations for the experiments. When Sultan takes in the whole situation and picks up a stick or a box, he is doing what he has observed the experimenter doing. He solves the problems presented him as designed by the men who provide the properties, the space, the incentive, and the model of whole response which Sultan employs in similar ways.

Those who reduce the nature of man to animal models distort and misperceive the greater capacity of man to achieve whole responses in meaningful perspectives. Likewise those who reduce the unconscious conflicts of id and superego to the conservation of energy in a closed system are misled by mechanical models of nineteenth-century physics. Our models need to keep pace with the advancing frontiers of science, and not be chained to the dogmas and the crudities of the past. When Freud began his study of man, he was caught in the machine age of medicine, as Frankl says. But he was not content to remain there.

We find persons living in several *dimensions*. To comprehend the intricate greatness of persons in all their multiple potentiality, we will need to recognize more than one dimension. If we seek with the sciences and theologies of the future to understand the emerging nature of man in truer perspective, we shall come to see him as a creature of many dimensions.

A pattern of levels once had meaning in the simple formulas of the past. The pyramid of matter-life-mind was a graphic portrayal. But matter is now seen as dynamic interaction of dancing electrons. And neither life nor mind is viewed in stationary or confining models of the past. Psychological depth is viewed by Freud beneath the conscious surface where the unconscious forces act and react in raging conflict. Yet unconscious wishes are penetrating all of life, as our behavior is revealed in "Freudian slips," unwitting errors, gestures, dreams, and actions.

However, the design of levels is too spatial and structural to convey the living dynamic of changing and growing life. We live on all levels at once, and these separations seem artificial, crude, and contrived. Such models are therefore being abandoned for a more free and interacting process of life moving out in many directions from an inner center, the self.

Dimensions are coordinates of a complex whole. We constantly perceive space in three dimensions and, since Einstein, a fourth dimension of time through which we move. Nothing is static as we naïvely assume, for every event is in time and all forces and planets are in motion. *E pluribus unum* is as true of personality as it is of nations, groups and individuals. We are not a collection but an interacting unity of diversity as an organism of interdependent relationships. The fallacy of most observations and theories of man is oversimplification. Whatever we see or think is fragmentary. And the whole is more than we have yet discovered or charted.

Rival schools of psychology and theology are like the blind men and the elephant in the well-known parable. Each one grasps but a part of the elephant and says: "I see the elephant is like a tree . . . a large leaf . . . a snake . . . a wall . . . a rope." Yet each one contributes some knowledge, though partial, to enrich the whole. The quarrel begins when each one assumes that he has the whole truth to defend against all other viewpoints. A dimensional view of personality will draw together partial views in a richer complexity of larger unifying wholeness.

If we consider the following circle diagram enclosing a cross, we have a mandala that appears in the religious art of Asia, Europe, and other cultures around the world.[23] This universal

---

[23] See Paul E. Johnson, *Personality and Religion* (Nashville: Abingdon Press, 1957), p. 233.

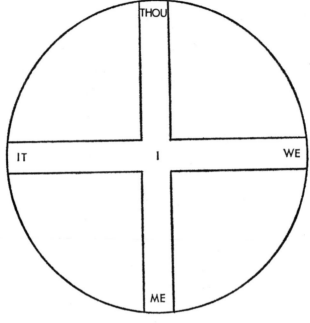

Dimensions of Personality

symbol, which Jung considers an archetype of the collective unconscious, may serve to point out four basic dimensions of personality. There are other dimensions no doubt; but this may
trace a ground plan of four magnetic interactions like the
directions of north, south, east, and west on the compass. The
Chinese, who invented the compass, noted a fifth point of this
magnetic field as the center where I stand.

Dimensions of personality meet and intersect at the center
of the person. For personality as we know it from within is an
intricate system of dynamic relationships whose focal center
is I—the subject of experience who observes and reaches out
in many directions. This unique self we recognize as the person
I am; the one who is aware of my living relationships through
all the dimensions that radiate from my personal experience.

The biotic dimension (I-ME) includes the many coordinating systems of my body in all the processes of life and growth. The spiritual dimension (I-THOU) is my search for the meaning, the value, and purpose of life in response to the Creative Mystery confronting us. The social dimension (I-WE) is my encounter with persons in the many relationships of life in our human community. The physical dimension (I-IT) is my ongoing interaction with the world to sustain and create our mutual potentiality.

The I actively participates in these dimensions simultaneously, yet in ever changing focus upon a whole spectrum of many-colored interests and concerns. This is our life—to participate through inflowing and outgoing interactions we have with the world of resources, organisms, persons, and values. Personality is an open system, constantly giving and receiving the vitalities and potentialities of life through enlarging consciousness.

Viktor Frankl has been showing us the larger meaning of a dimensional psychology and ontology.[24] To his existential analysis the meaning of life is an encounter. Self-actualization is like the pursuit of pleasure, a merely empty and futile confinement to a self-centered existence. Meaning is realized in our response to other persons and events in the concrete situation confronting us. The uniquely human dimension is the spirit, the subject I, who can be aware of the challenge life brings in each moment and who is free to decide how I will respond. When we are able to be creative, we contribute to fulfillment of life with other persons. If our powers are limited by illness or confining circumstance, we may yet experience love and beauty in values shared with other persons. In acute suffering there is a new challenge to meet the stress of this situation bravely, without giving up to despair, but calling forth the inherent nobility of the spirit. Thus every person may find meaning in whatever life asks of him, even to the last breath.

Teilhard and Frankl converge on the noosphere as the grow-

---

[24] See all of his writings, and particularly his *Will to Meaning*.

ing edge of man and our planet in the onward course of this unfolding into the future. And they both see man's spirit as but one dimension of life in relation to the physical, biological, and social interactions of our multiple encounter with this world.

Rising spiritually above one's own psychophysical condition might also be called the existential act. By this very act man opens and enters the noölogical dimension of being; nay, even creates this dimension as a dimension of his own. But this does not in the least detract from the fact that humans and animals have the biological and psychological dimensions in common.[25]

We are not speaking of layers or levels of being. For that would disrupt the wholeness of life into segments to separate from one another. But if we understand body, psyche, and spirit as inseparable dimensions of one being, the wholeness of growing life is affirmed in all its emerging directions.

A dimensional psychology and theology provide many vistas of insight and foresight through which to perceive the greatness of our life as persons. We have looked at some of these in this chapter. Other vistas and revelations will open to us as we continue our journey with each other as persons, who seek to grow in the perspectives of expanding faith and knowledge.

---

[25] Frankl, *The Will to Meaning*, p. 137.

Two: Expansion of Personal Consciousness

V

The Sense of Sensitivity

We began the introduction to this book by saying man's central problem is alienation. We have discussed briefly some of the causes of his alienation. We have said that even those who have presumed to help man overcome his alienation have resorted to methods spun out of scientific presuppositions which have actually contributed to his problem. This kind of circular process needs seriously to be examined and changed. We have acknowledged that changes are occurring as people are becoming acutely conscious of their consciousness. Since alienation is a deadening of sensitivity, hopefully the awakening to consciousness is bringing sensitivity to life.

Having thus placed a premium on sensitivity, we must say what we mean by the term. We must make explicit the dynamics of a truly sensitive person by concentrating on what makes him so.

In popular language the word "sensitivity" is usually immediately associated with the group movement which has swept across the country during recent years. In that context the term has been either much heralded or much maligned, depending upon whether the people involved felt they were benefited or harmed by the experience. Some who have never actually been in such groups have picked up whatever negative material that has come from participants and have made the movement a scapegoat for their negative feelings. The ways in which sensitivity experiences can be legitimately criticized get obscured in the gross generalizations which are made.

Carl Rogers has aptly characterized some of the prevailing attitudes toward sensitivity groups:

Most universities still look upon it with scorn. Until the last two or three years, foundations and government agencies have been unwilling to fund programs of research in this area; the established professions of clinical psychology and psychiatry have stayed aloof, while the political right wing is certain that it represents a deep-seated communist plot. I know of few other trends which have so clearly expressed the need and desire of *people* rather than institutions.[1]

Implicitly in this statement Rogers has not only taken note of the burgeoning interest in sensitivity groups but also reinforced the theme of this book: namely, that the "needs and desires of people" be given high priority.

What is meant by the term "sensitivity"? The probability is extremely high that the bad name it has received has been caused by people who have not been able to give it a proper translation, either conceptually or operationally. We are not necessarily arguing in favor of sensitivity groups as such, but we are definitely taking a stand for sensitivity to persons. In fact, we regard the act of sensitizing persons basic to moral and ethical behavior.

We interpret Talcott Parsons to be giving a significant notion of the meaning of sensitivity, by inference, in the following:

Consideration of the conditions on which . . . a stable, mutually oriented system of interaction depends leads to the conclusion that on the human level . . . mutuality of interaction must be mediated and stabilized by a common culture—that is, by a commonly shared system of symbols, the meanings of which are understood on both sides with an approximation to agreement. . . . It may be presumed that the prominence of common symbol systems is both a consequence and a condition of the extreme plasticity and sensitivity of the human organism, which in turn are essential conditions of its capacities to learn, and, concomitantly, to mislearn.[2]

[1] *Carl Rogers on Encounter Groups*, p. 2.
[2] "The Superego and the Theory of Social Systems," in Norman W. Bell and Ezra Vogel, eds., *A Modern Introduction to the Family* (rev. ed.; New York: Free Press, 1968), p. 686.

1. *Internalization*

Parsons makes this statement in the context of a discussion of how a person internalizes social systems in the development of what classical psychoanalysis has termed the "superego." Freud had seen the superego as the source of moral anxiety in the person. We refer to this material because we feel that it points to the derivation of moral sensitivity, which begins originally with the complex system of symbols which develop between a mother and her infant. This is the prototype for developing sensitivity. We shall examine this in detail.

This is quite a different view from that of Freud, who saw the superego as a product of the internalized ("introjected values") parent. The superego became an essential part of the personality itself, and distinct from the ego. In fact, Parsons rightly distinguishes that Freud was making "an unreal separation between the ego and the superego."

The reason Freud fell into such a dichotomous position is: He took "external reality" as a given, failing to recognize that any frame of reference in which things are understood is cultural and is internalized. Assuming that the ego was responding to external reality and the superego was internalizing by identification, Freud tended to separate the two. He seemed to be ignoring the fact that the culture is internalized as well and directly affects the child's interpretation of what things mean.

> Moral standards . . . cannot . . . be dissociated from the content of the orientation patterns which they regulate. . . . Neither what the human object *is* in the most significant respects, nor what it *means* emotionally, can be understood as given independently of the nature of the interactive process itself; and the significance of moral norms themselves very largely relates to this fact.[3]

What the mother is to the child and what she *means* to him, comes out of the process of interaction between them. They are united also in the common culture which has much to say about how they understand and feel toward each other.

The second significant factor in the development of moral

---

[3] *Ibid.*, p. 687.

discernment and sensitivity concerns a transition in the relationship of the child to his mother. Parsons sees this as the reciprocal love attitude which develops between the mother and the child.

Moving beyond Freud's notion of erotic gratification (the child's cathexis—attachment or aversion—toward the mother), we see the developing of a symbol system to the point where the mother's *attitude* becomes of critical importance to the child. She takes on special *meaning* for the child. She is no longer just meeting his needs for physical gratification. She is a unique *someone* to him. He is now depending on the *love* of his mother and not just on what she does for him. He is learning how to love as well as how to be loved.

> The child must mature to the point where he can play a responsible role in a system of social interaction, where he can understand that what people feel is a function of his and their conformity with mutually held standards of conduct. *Only when he has become dependent on his mother's love can he develop meaningful anxiety, in that then he might jeopardize his security in that love by not living up to her expectations of being a good boy.*[4]

Thus, the developing moral sensitivity of the child, or to use Freud's category, the superego, is dependent upon the *social system* of interaction building up between the mother and her child. In this relationship he begins to internalize the culture and to create patterns which affect further relationships. We will say more about this in connection with our discussion of his integration of what he internalizes later in this chapter.

A prime illustration of the internalized common culture is the process of learning the sex role. The presumably constitutionally given duality of sexual orientation, which Freud seemed to be emphasizing, is extremely questionable. There is no strong evidence to support definite biologically constituted sexuality. In fact, much more credence is being given to the assumption that sex differences are largely psychological and are learned from the culture.

---

[4] *Ibid.,* p. 691. Italics added.

2. Differentiation

The necessity and the problem of differentiation are especially seen in the differences in sex and social roles in the highly differentiated social system of the United States. Early anthropological data had lent credence to the view that there is considerable variance between the activities of the husband and wife. Morris Zelditch, Jr., in a study of fifty-six societies, has taken the opposite view; namely, despite differences in particular activities, there is a general principle of differentiation between the sexes. He identifies the two roles as adaptive-instrumental and expressive-integrative.[5]

Usually, the father is primarily involved in the adaptive-instrumental role, which is task-oriented and requires engaging in activities "out there" or "at work" and manipulation of the object world. However, all other members of the family engage in adaptive-instrumental activities and in so doing are *dispersed* for a period of time. If they were not reunited, the system would break down; hence the expressive-integrative side is required. Usually, the mother is symbolizing the expressive-integrative behavior, although the intention here is not necessarily to imply that such roles should be always identified with the sex role.

Characteristic of the adaptive-instrumental leader is the tendency to behave rationally toward the external situation (in order to control it better) and to inhibit emotions toward other members of the family (for example, to accept hostile feelings from another, again perhaps for the sake of order and control). On the other hand, the expressive-integrative leader, as the phrase implies, tends to express emotions to others, give supportive behavior, desires to please and to be liked. Zelditch labels the first "task leader" and the second, "sociometric star." Surely the meaning of the former is obvious. The latter refers to the person who stands out in expressive and supportive qualities.

[5] "Role Differentiation in the Nuclear Family: A Comparative Study," in *ibid.*, pp. 346-48.

Common to both roles and of critical significance is not, as may be supposed, the physical acts of going out or being there but the basic attitudes and behaviors which characterize the different roles. Changes in attitudes and behavior which occur in the transition from one state to the other are essential if the family system is to survive. Either the family is integrated regularly or their preoccupation with tasks disintegrates them. "We can say, then, that the system [family] must differentiate behaviors and attitudes in order to exist as a system; and that a further condition of stability is also that some specialization occur in responsibility for the attitudes and behaviors involved." [6]

The integrative-expressive leader cannot be involved in task-oriented activities all the time. Some relief is needed from too much occupation with either instrumental-adaptive attitudes and behavior or those of the integrative-expressive nature. The laughing, playing, expressing of warmth for others, which are integrative-expressive attitudes and behavior, can no more be endlessly tolerated than can the achievement-oriented, emotion-inhibited attitudes and behavior of the instrumental-adaptive role.

The women's liberation movement is undoubtedly a healthy revolt against the mechanization of sex-role differentiation. Members of the so-called "lib" group rebel at being discriminated against in a sex-role differentiation which is sharply categorical. Undoubtedly, by mutual understanding and agreement, roles, as defined, can be exchanged by the husband and wife. The critical point is: Someone must be taking responsibility for the instrumental, decision-making role at a particular time, while the other is assuming an integrative, supportive, and expressive role. The usual expectation is that the male adult will take the role of instrumental leader, while the female becomes the expressive leader.

The major point here is that every child learns his sex role by internalizing the culture's interpretations of sex-role differ-

[6] *Ibid.*, p. 349.

entiation. It should be evident that seeing the sex role as biologically constituted is to project one's own views on it, for whatever advantage the viewer may be seeking to gain! Sex-role differentiation is a *learned* phenomenon, not a given. The implications for moral and ethical behavior are numerous and are the subject of intense discussions among men and women who are battling against subtle and obvious forms of sexual domination.

3. Identification

Our discussion leads us to the problem of identification. The term now needs to be redefined in the light of what we have just said. We continue to affirm, with Freud, that identification is the principal activity in the development of the superego. However, we now must see it as the internalization of the common culture. That is, the way we talk about things, the expression of our feelings about them, and our system of moral norms form the common culture which the child internalizes.

The Freudian view of the psychosexual development of the child stressed his differentiating himself from the parent of the opposite sex and identifying with the parent of the same sex. Of course, differentiation from the parent of the same sex occurs also. In the so-called "Oedipal period" (which psychoanalysts regard as encompassing the period roughly from about two and one-half to five), for example, the girl differentiates from her mother and attaches to her father as "love object." She later represses her feelings for her father and identifies with her mother.

Lidz notes a similar pattern in the development of the boy:

A harmonious relationship between the parents, in which the mother loves and respects her husband as a man and supports him in his masculine roles, permits the boy to develop a harmonious self-structure. The person with whom he identifies is desirable to the person who is his primary love object; and by following his paternal model he gains self-esteem in feeling that he can be loved and wanted. The same considerations apply to the girl.[7]

Lidz recognizes that his statement is rather idealistic and that reality is something quite short of this. However, he is affirming the validity of the identification process and arguing for the coalition between parents which makes identification possible. Resolution of the oedipal conflict depends upon a degree of success in identifying with the parent of the same sex, thus increasing the child's self-esteem.

Now, however we feel that Parsons' view rightly implies it is just as proper to speak of the boy's learning his sex role by identification with his mother as with his father. He learns sex categorization from her because he discovers how he and she belong to different sex categories. Of course, the same is true of the girl in relation to her father.

Identification is more than a psychosexual phenomenon. Groups and causes which claim the loyalties of people influence the personal identity of those who give such loyalties. The person who belongs to a group tends to be moved by the expectations of members of that group to behave in ways acceptable to the group. In fact, the person's behavior will usually vary considerably, depending upon the group with which he is presently associating. For this reason, one can never deal with the individual in isolation as though he were a "windowless monad," but always must see him as a part of the system, or a system within a system, and so on.

If a person identifies with another person or group to the extent of participation, he is thus affirming himself. In that sense, identification is an act of self-affirmation. However, to identify may also seem to be an act of self-denial, especially if such action comes out of deep self-hatred, which usually is not conducive to genuine participation anyway.

Tillich has shown that manifestations of "the courage to be as a part" are exhibited in collectivist, neocollectivist, and dem-

---

[7] Theodore Lidz, *The Person* (New York, Basic Books, 1968), p. 231.

ocratic conformist forms.[8] In collectivist societies the test of membership is in the courage to take pain and death and to accept guilt as public guilt. Identification with the group is complete. The system breaks down because it obscures the demands for personal contrition which makes for responsible participation in any society.

Neocollectivist movements (i.e., Nazism, Fascism, Communism) differ from the older collectivist mode in the "liberation of autonomous reason and the creation of a technical civilization." To maintain the system a strong centralized, technical organization is developed, and alternatives or individual decisions are suppressed. Yet, similar to the older collectivist societies, the fundamental notion of participation is maintained. Individual expressiveness of members of the group (such as through the media of art and literature) is prohibited. The neocollectivist's "sin," however it may be interpreted, is against the collective. He confesses to the collective and accepts the judgment and punishment of the collective. Forgiveness is from the collective and his promise of transformation is directed there.

Participation in the system of democratic conformity is based on the belief in the creative individual as a "unique representative of the universal"—a belief which gave rise to considerable emphasis on production (this is especially true of American society). "Participation in the productive process demands conformity and adjustment to the ways of social production.[9]

We may conclude that identification is an internalization of the common culture, not just a parent or parents. Cultural patterns are incorporated into the personality. A cultural pattern, the way one cuts his hair or wears his clothes, gets attached with emotional significance. Indeed, a person's whole self-concept is affected by his positive or negative feelings about cultural patterns he has internalized.

[8] *The Courage to Be* (New Haven: Yale University Press, 1952), pp. 90-112.
[9] *Ibid.*, p. 112.

4. Integration

If a person is to interact fully with his culture, he must bring his feelings and the cultural patterns he is internalizing into an integrated whole.

The principal mechanism by which this is accomplished appears to be through the building up of attachments to other persons—that is, by emotional communication with others so that the individual is *sensitized to the attitudes of the others,* not merely to their specific acts with their intrinsic gratification-deprivation significance.[10]

A person becomes socialized as he is able to integrate his understanding of emotional meanings and their expression with his conceptualization of objects and with his system of moral norms by which he relates to others. All of these are internalized and make up the content of the personality.

"A mature and workable personality integration is not achieved simply through nurturance of inborn directives and potentialities but requires positive direction and guidance in a suitable interpersonal environment and social system."[11]

The suitability of an interpersonal environment and social system which facilitates the integrating thrust of each person is the subject of our concern here.

As Lidz proceeds to point out, every person needs to grow up in a family (or reasonable substitute), not only for protection and nurturance during his early years of great dependency, but also to be directed to be an integrating person who assimilates techniques necessary for adaptation and survival. Also he must "internalize the institutions and roles of structured social systems as well as identify with persons who themselves have assimilated the culture."[12]

Expanding awareness requires understanding and appropriating the meaning of the past. It is not the result of the total

[10] Parsons, "The Superego and the Theory of Social Systems," p. 692.
[11] Lidz, *The Person,* p. 67.
[12] *Ibid.*

abandonment of discipline or contempt for history, as some contemporary behavior would imply. "Doing one's own thing" may not at all be an act of creativity or spontaneity but of irresponsibility, especially if it is largely imitative, as it often is, thus becoming a palpably self-contradictory phrase. The basic intent of the idea is valid. The act of breaking out of conventional patterns of behavior which have crystallized around unquestioned, unexamined group mores is imperative to creating new vitality and meaning. However, if it is not done in responsible relationship to the past and with appreciation for what has been received, it comes out as self-indulgent parasitism.

Norman Cousins has observed:

> The cultural atmosphere in general is far from nourishing as the child grows older. Honest experimentation in the arts, always essential, is being seriously weakened by ignorance of or contempt for the past. An epidemic of imitativeness is enfeebling the development of necessary new techniques and perceptions. Shoddiness and ineptness are disguised as legitimate exercises in subjectivity or expressionism. The total result is hardly a triumph for creativity or the rational process.[18]

A distinction should be made here between "expressionism" and the "expressive" mode. Expressionism refers to expressing for its own sake, without necessarily regarding how it affects others. Expressive leadership draws out expressive responses from other members of the community, and tends to integrate the community. Expressionism affirms the self, whereas expressive relating affirms others and strengthens their resolve to be and to become.

The expressive mode requires a sense of history and destiny. Rejoicing in the traditions which give solidarity to the family, but being open to new experiences which change these traditions, the family periodically celebrates its life and gives significant recognition to its members. For the nuclear family, such

[18] Editorial, "The Taming of Individuals and the State," *Saturday Review*, January 17, 1970, p. 26.

reuniting may occur every evening at the dinner hour. The extended family may get together only now and then or on special occasions.

Integrating moves beyond identifying. A responsible mode of relating to persons and events is required. One does not achieve integration simply by taking on the symbols of a creative process. The very stuff of creativity must come from him, which implies a deeply sensitized response to reality. In so doing, he contributes creatively to the systems which comprise him and of which he is a part. These include not only the external world but also the common culture.

We have used three illustrations—sex-role differentiation, identification, and integration to show ways in which mechanistic interpretations of the person are inadequate. We have said they are inadequate because they ignore the reality of social systems. The person who adapts a caricature of a mechanistic position says, in effect, "I am not spontaneous, because I have a tyrannous superego!" He is admitting the compartmentalization which is allowed by that position, but he is ignoring dimensions of that very superego which we have been identifying here.

Sensitivity is increased as the person engages in emotional communications with others. In this way he becomes deeply aware of the attitudes of others, not just their isolated acts which are either gratifying or depriving in their effect upon him. As each becomes aware of the attitudes of the other, they build up a common culture of shared symbols. This is the process of socialization by which people are enabled to live together in rich and meaningful associations. A reductionist culture tends to separate and alienate. In such a culture people yearn for the trust relationships by which they are created and through which they create. Such experiences infuse their lives with new meaning and purpose.

Each age level of life brings new opportunities for expanding and deepening the person's awareness. We will next look in detail at the nature of the common culture which makes up each epoch of the life cycle.

VI

The Drama of Personal Development

We have considered the origins of a personality as a developing and changing system. We said the system begins as a complex pattern of interaction which develops between a mother and her child. The transactions taking place between them make up an emerging "symbol system" in which each learns to anticipate and effect changes in the other. The way the child comes to regard his environment, the way he feels about himself and others, the words he uses to describe things and events, the values he gives to objects, the terms he employs to express his feelings and values—all become part of this elaborate symbol system.

The child soon moves into the process of clearing up whatever distortions have muddied up his perceptions. He is getting into focus what Harry Stack Sullivan has called his "parataxic distortions." [1] That is, he is evaluating his perceptions alongside those of other people and seeking to find "consensual validation" for his symbols. Does a smiling face always mean good intentions toward him? If a person says "no" to him, does that mean he doesn't like him? And so on.

He is learning to reflect upon his experiences and to make logical connections between them. If his logic breaks down, he tends to revise his notions, expecially if he is free enough emotionally to be open to learning possibilities. A high measure of self-esteem reinforced by the esteem of significant people

[1] *Interpersonal Theory of Psychiatry* (New York: Norton, 1953), p. 305.

around him helps him in this regard. He now begins to develop what Sullivan termed "the syntaxic mode," which may be best described as a strong correlation between his concepts and reality. Thus, he learns to make his own decisions and to be responsible for them.

Each person's symbol system contains main developmental themes which become critical at given stages of his life. We will now give attention to what we regard as the central themes of each epoch in the life cycle.

The contributions of developmental theorists such as Sullivan, Jean Piaget, Erik Erikson, and others have been revolutionary and liberating. They have freed scholars from dependence upon mechanistic views of man. However, they are being revised and changed as we discover more about the inner world of man.

Rudolf Dreikurs, for example, takes issue with any presumed orthodoxy in the notion of developmental sequences. In his discussion of an educational climate which would take seriously the self-concept and the basic motivation of the child in realizing the child's own potential, Dreikurs says:

It has been suggested that children could, within the first ten years, acquire all the knowledge presently obtained through higher education. Until most recently this was considered unrealistic, wishful thinking. The question has been and still is being raised whether such development would be desirable or harmful. During the past few years new observations have been made with increased frequency which seem to substantiate the assumption that early learning is not detrimental.[2]

Dreikurs is not arguing that parents should put the pressure on their children, a child training approach which the "developmentalists" decried. On the contrary, Dreikurs advocates parental reinforcement of the learning which is already going on. The fundamental problem is: Neither parents nor teachers are tremendously skillful in encouraging children in their own

[2] "Development of the Child's Potential," in Herbert Otto, ed., *Explorations in Human Potentialities* (Springfield, Ill.: Charles C. Thomas, 1966), pp. 233-34.

decision-making. The recognition that the child can decide and is deciding opens up the possibilities for responsible growth. However, this can happen only if we truly believe it.

If development is viewed strictly from a cause-effect perspective, it is misleading and can be used to excuse behavior or to categorize a person. Both these tendencies actually rob the person of his creativity and essential humanity. Yet in order to understand a person's contemporary struggle toward self-actualization, some knowledge of his development is extremely important.

On the other hand, what he thinks and believes *now* influences his behavior. He is making decisions, changing his concepts, and setting goals in interaction with his peers and the adults around him. If he receives the encouragement he needs, he may, through his decisions, expedite his development. In any event, children actually do decide whether they will cooperate in a learning process or not. If they are motivated and become interested, their learning capacities are actually rather fantastic.

The decisions a child makes profoundly affect his development. The child's capacity to make these decisions, in turn, is greatly influenced by the symbol system which develops between the child and his parents. If the parent esteems his child, the child develops a positive self-esteem. The great tragedy in the lack of respect is not that the child will suffer some kind of pathology (which is a compartmentalizing form of thinking), but that he will realize far less of his potential than he otherwise might.

Bearing in mind, therefore, that development and decision are in a potentially creative tension in every moment of experiencing, we will examine in detail the developmental stages in the life cycle from birth to death. Theodore Lidz' commentary on the contributions of Erikson and Piaget and his own organization of the stages will serve as a guide and a model.[3]

[3] Lidz, *The Person.*

Lidz regards *infancy* as approximately the first fifteen months of life (allowing for individual variations), when the baby can neither walk nor talk and is quite dependent on others for total care. The *toddler* stage begins when the child learns to walk. At this time the child begins to be able to get himself into situations which he can neither understand nor control. Consequently, he needs limits set by his parents. However, parental control sets off conflict between that control and desire for initiative on the part of the child.

During the *oedipal period*, roughly four and five, the child is discovering his place as a boy or girl in the family. The child revises eroticized parental attachments to enable him to move into peer relationships. The *juvenile* period is a time of finding acceptance in peer groups and discovering that he "can do"; he has skills which earn him a place with his peers. He also begins to discern what other people are like and, at the same time, develops an image of himself.

Adolescence is characterized as a time of tension between sexual maturation and incomplete physical maturity, as well as conflict between dependency and independency. One of the chief tasks of an adolescent is to become responsibly independent of his family. In the period of *young adulthood* personality changes are dramatically effected by occupational and marital choices and reoriented by parenthood, with its growing responsibilities.

The *middle years* are marked by considerable "stock taking," since the opportunities for a radical reorganization are diminishing. In most cases, children are no longer the central preoccupation of the parents, who are now facing each other and perhaps struggling with realigning their relationship. In *older maturity* physical abilities are becoming increasingly limited. Bereavement and losses of many kinds become pronounced. Retirement forces reorientation of the persons' lives. They tend to become more or less dependent upon others for basic needs.[4]

The foregoing developmental stages and the struggles of

[4] *Ibid.*, pp. 75-76.

creative growth typical of each will be discussed below as follows: Infancy and Childhood (Trust-Initiative), Adolescence (Independence-Relationship), Young Adulthood (Compassion-Fidelity), and Older Maturity (Creativity-Community).[5]

1. Infancy and Childhood: Trust-Initiative

Every person needs self-esteem. He struggles his whole life to get it, to maintain, and to increase it. He gets self-esteem from the basic communities which nourish him. He maintains it in relation to communities whose acceptance he values. He increases it as he serves the communities which are significant to him. The foundations for self-esteem are laid in infancy, not in a deterministic sense, but in a realistically effective way.

The infant's developing symbol system is now expanding to include other members of his family, whether nuclear or extended. He learns who grandmother, grandfather, uncle, aunt, and other relatives are. He builds up meanings of the words from his various experiences of relating to them.

If his parents accept the child in themselves responsibly, they communicate to the child it is safe for him to be. Thus, they encourage his spontaneity and cooperation. From his mother, initially, and from his father, the child learns how to love.

Receiving and Trusting

The critical task of the infant and the main theme of his early development is that of developing feelings of confidence in the world. He is depending on others, probably largely unwittingly, but increasingly he needs to be assured that those upon whom he depends are dependable.

Erik Erikson has named the central task of infancy, *basic trust*, as contrasted with mistrust of others and the world. He states the dynamics of this stage as "getting what is given" and "getting somebody to do something for him" as the groundwork for identifying with the giver and "getting to be" the giver. He calls this the incorporative stage.

[5] See Erik Erikson, *Childhood and Society* (New York: Norton, 1950).

In regard to the implications of Erikson's views for the Christian community, which is, after all, the context for this whole discussion of personality development, we quote the concluding paragraph of the section on basic trust: "Whoever says he has religion must derive a faith from it which is transmitted to infants in the form of basic trust; whoever claims that he has not the need for religion must derive such basic faith from elsewhere." [6]

The parents' perspectives upon life and its meaning infuse their whole being and affects everything they do. Their attitudes and feelings are profoundly influenced, of course, by how they see and experience the world. This basic outlook is transmitted to the child and deeply affects his experiencing of the world. Their openness and genuineness, all moods and attitudes, are communicated to the child.

2. Toddler: Venturing Forth

As the child becomes ambulatory, he explores the world by sticking himself into all kinds of situations. His curiosity exceeds his capacity to handle what he gets himself into, but is powerfully conducive to his knowledge of the world. The carnival operator, the concessionaire, the used-car dealer, or the exhibitor at a grand opening knows the value of the high-powered, beacon-type, arc light to attract people for miles around to his showing. Or, when the "wet paint" sign is displayed in a public building, are we not tempted to test its authenticity by touching it? (Perhaps yielding to this temptation originated the popular pastime of finger painting!) Likewise, the *toddler* projects himself into every situation possible to experience and to authenticate the world in which he lives. He is putting together the words he learns with what they symbolize, and getting a "feel for both."

The toddler is beginning to develop ideas about himself and

[6] "Growth and Crises in Healthy Personality," in Kluckhohn, Clyde, Murray *et al.*, eds., *Personality in Nature, Society, and Culture* (New York: Knopf, 1954), p. 197.

his world. Such ideation is highly idiosyncratic; i. e., he is constructing an image of himself and his world which is peculiar to him. Thus he is able to internalize the world, as he sees it, and to manage it. He is not yet particularly concerned about whether other people experience the world as he does.

Symbolizing and Learning

He is also beginning to make symbolic representations about his world. He experiments with objects and observes their action. He watches falling objects and carefully traces their path. Piaget has reported that a child of a little more than one year of age watched him remove and put back the top of his tobacco jar. Although the child was close enough to reach the jar, and perhaps to imitate the action, she was satisfied to raise her hand and lower it in gestures simulating Piaget's motions, without touching the jar. She was symbolizing through gestures what she was observing. As the child is able increasingly to symbolize in this way, he is being transformed from a private individual to a social one. He can now begin to communicate with others and with himself. He constructs ideas about which he can think and remember. "His knowledge, then, can begin to transcend immediate events. Meaning becomes the way in which he represents events to himself." [7]

From about eighteen months to two years of age, the child is undergoing a significant transition from an internally directed and organized organism to a social being. He is enabled in his social interaction by the development of his capacity to symbolize events. By symbolizing what he is experiencing, he breaks down into meaningful events what is presented to him. He is able to distinguish one part of an event from another. If a yellow bus is moving along a freeway, he can now begin to distinguish the color "yellow" from the action "moving" from the place where the action is happening, along a freeway.

[7] From a report on Jean Piaget's experiments with children in *Psychology Today*, (Del Mar, Calif.: CRM Books, 1970), pp. 189-190.

Substages in Symbol Work

Three substages in this "symbol work" of the child are: the *naturalistic*, the *intuitive*, and the *concrete*.[8] The naturalistic substage is evident in the child from about one and a half to four years of age. The child represents events playfully and imitatively. He does not yet use conventional symbols to talk about an event. He often uses human-action metaphors. For example, recently when I skimmed a flat rock across a small pond, a three-year-old boy standing nearby shouted, "Oh, look at him hop, and jump, and dive in!" Children also imitate the speech they hear, but put it in words sometimes understandable only to them and their immediate family. My granddaughter at the age of two and a half called for a drink of water by saying "awkawa." However, this could also mean a request for orange juice, tomato juice, milk, or any of a number of liquids she was used to getting. One had to know the context in order to get the meaning. (Her grandmother had an uncanny grasp of what was being communicated, for she usually produced the right beverage!)

The intuitive substage involves the degree to which the child sees himself as the center of what he is experiencing. He regards what happens as the result of his actions. He may feel that the sun is following him around, etc. He interprets events in the light of how they affect him. His immediate experiences are primary. However, he is beginning to distinguish things and to recognize they do not change strictly in relation to him. He sees that they have their own identity. Last summer, as we were traveling in the mountains, I (LGC) asked my five-year-old daughter if the mountains were getting larger as we moved closer to them. "Oh no, Daddy," she quickly replied in a tone which almost had a note of disgust in it, "they just look bigger because we are getting closer to them." She gestured matter of factly as if to say, "Any fool knows that!"

The concrete substage may be introduced as follows: "The child achieves relatively full understanding of the concrete, but

[8] *Ibid.*, pp. 191-96.

not abstract actualities of his physical environment and the concrete conventions of his social environment during the period of about seven to twelve years of age." [9] A child now begins to classify objects and to differentiate their physical qualities. He becomes flexible in his understanding of events. He does not insist that things are as he sees them, but is more open to different ways of viewing them. Also he can distinguish better that changes in happenings occur and can be reversed. A familiar experiment with children in this regard involves the placing of an equal amount of water in different sizes of containers and having the child judge which container has the greatest amount of water. Children in the intuitive substage will select the container which appears to have more water (the long narrow cylinder versus the short wide glass), while those in the concrete substage know the amounts are the same.[10]

The beginning of disengagements from parents is the source of religious growth for the four- and five-year-old child. The child is beginning to get himself and his world in perspective. He is perceiving the relative size of things. Some he sees as very small and some as large. He is developing a sense of wonder and mystery about life. He is learning about people and placing them in the larger cosmic context.

The child is greatly concerned to understand the actual character of events. His increasing capacity to do so helps him in his struggle to perceive accurately and become effective in his social interactions. The elementary levels of moral discrimination are emerging in the concrete stage. The child is becoming conscious of standards of justice. He is aware of and is increasingly sensitive to injustices he sees toward others. He can perceive concretely the external evidences of unfair treatment, but he is not yet capable of transcending himself sufficiently to discern injustices toward him. Also, he is not yet secure enough in his relationships to become that critical of others. Nevertheless, he is developing the capacity to become

[9] *Ibid.*, p. 194.
[10] *Ibid.*, pp. 194-95.

morally indignant at perceived wrongs. The foundations of his sense of social justice are being laid.

3. The Oedipal Period: Becoming a Boy or Girl

The Oedipal stage in the preschool child is the time the child finds himself in the family as a boy or girl. Freud made much of this phase, basing his assumptions on what he believed was the universal validity of the Oedipus myth. Oedipus in the Greek legend was the tragic hero who had slain his father, the king, and had incestuous relations with his mother, not knowing either were his parents. Freud saw this myth as describing the eroticized attachments of four- and five-year-olds to the parent of the opposite sex. Conflict occurs, Freud observed, as the child competes with the parent of the same sex for the love and affection of the other parent. The child also struggles to identify with the parent of the same sex to snatch the power and prerogatives which belong to that parent.

Psychoanalysts have asserted that sexual identity is determined by the resolution of the Oedipal situation. If the child is able to differentiate himself or herself from the parent of the opposite sex, and identify strongly with the person of the same sex, he is able to work out an appropriate psychosexual identity. Another part of the struggle involves the development of conscience. As the Oedipal conflict is resolved and the guilt which goes along with it is handled, the child acquires a sense of moral responsibility. As he learns the social rules regarding such differentiation and identification—how one behaves as a male or female in relation to members of the same and opposite sex in his family—he represses Oedipal desires and resolves the conflict.

Anthropologists have found that the Oedipal situation does not exist in all societies, especially in those which do not tie the family unit with biological parents. Therefore, on that ground the Oedipal situation is not seen as a universal developmental phenomenon. The struggle for sex-role development, however, apparently is a universal phenomenon. The question of what is a sex role appropriate to the male and female is yet a debated one. Some argue that basic role distinctions should be made,[11] others that they are too sharply drawn. The controversy will be discussed at several subsequent points in later chapters of this book.

The struggle for autonomy and the development of initiative are aided by parental encouragement. Mutual respect of parent and child engenders such development. The child's capacity for moral judgment is thus increased. He is now ready to begin appraising his situation of dependency. Engagement with his parents and family in the dependency-independency struggle, his chief preoccupation in adolescence, is beginning to occur.

Encouraging Integrity

Erikson, Piaget, and others who have contributed classic studies to the understanding of human development have dealt with the dynamics of the growing child but have said little about the appropriate responsiveness of parents. Perhaps this is assumed. However, if those who insist we may be keeping our children babies too long are to be heeded, some explicit attention to parental responsibility needs to be given. Dreikurs, for example, argues that children not only need basically to trust their parents, but also to receive trust from them.

Trust does not imply a laissez-faire attitude, but a fundamental belief in the worthiness of the other—"the belief in his strength and ability, both to contribute and to stand up under adversities." [12] Trust cannot be a mask for indifference and disinterest. "I trust him," as an excuse for irresponsible non-involvement with a child is a contradiction. Trust is a positive, active, concerned expression of belief in the other, reflecting the integrity of attitude and action of the trusting one. Nor is it blind to situations where trust obviously is not merited. However, children today have shown they can and do decide for themselves. Parents strengthen their relationship with their

[11] Bell and Vogel, *The Family*, pp. 345-55.
[12] Dreikurs, "Development of the Child's Potential," p. 225.

children by supporting and encouraging them in this decision-making process.

4. The Juvenile Period: Gaining Self-Confidence

The juvenile phase of the life cycle is a time of the child's learning democratic interaction with his peers. With his departure to school, he leaves the comparative security of the family constellation and embarks on a strange and sometimes frightening adventure in the social world. He meets and makes new friends. He competes with them to get a sense of his power and achievement. He now begins to invest his energies and talents largely outside the home, learning to get along with his peers.

Freud termed this phase the "latency period" because he assumed it was the time of relative calm between the Oedipal phase and adolescent development. Libidinal drives were believed to be subsiding. There is no real evidence that sexual interests do, in fact, become diminished. However, such concentration of attention on outside interests prevails that the child is virtually taken "outside of himself" with less attention to his bodily functions.

Erikson has characterized the juvenile era as a time when the chief developmental task is industry, the awareness of the child that he can do and accomplish. Failure at this time results in feelings of inferiority and inadequacy. Piaget marks the juvenile phase as the period when the child is developing his *moral judgment*. He is moving from a *morality of constraint* to a *morality of cooperation*. During the earlier years in the development of his sense of justice, the child is ruled by the morality of constraint. He feels that the same punishment should be meted out for an offense, regardless of the circumstances. After about the tenth year he usually progresses into a morality of cooperation, which takes into account the motivation and the social implication of acts. He is becoming more discriminating in his moral judgments.

The "chum" is significant toward the end of this period of development, as Harry Stack Sullivan shows. A trusting and abiding relationship with a special friend of the same sex enables both to discover more of themselves and to draw out each other. "In the succeeding phase of preadolescence, in the company of one's chum, one finds oneself more and more able to talk about things which one had learned during the juvenile era not to talk about." [13]

Also he is learning democracy by the power struggles in which he engages as well as those which he is beginning to discern going on about him. He is discovering that he cannot push people around, without expecting to get pushed around in return. He is also learning that he is stronger than some people and weaker than others, both physically and mentally. Furthermore, he is beginning to develop ways of compensating for one or the other. These experiences and others beyond the family orientation help him to overcome his self-centeredness and family preoccupations. He becomes free to begin his unifying operations, which are essential to his social, intellectual, and ethical development.

5. Adolescence: Struggling for Independence

I see no hope for the future of our people if they are dependent on the frivolous youth of today, for certainly all youth are reckless beyond words. When I was a boy, we were taught to be discreet and respectful of elders, but the present youth are exceedingly wise and impatient of restraint.

Is this a quote from an editorial page of one of our modern newspapers? Or a letter from a harried contemporary parent of a teen-ager? Or a cynical outcry from a distraught educator in one of his less controlled moments of despair? In fact, the words are from none of these. They were attributed to Hesiod, the Greek poet who wrote in the eighth century B.C. Yet they have a sound which may ring familiar to modern parents and teachers. They show that the so-called generation gap is an age-old phenomenon and hardly unique to the present day. Modern youth are less frivolous and more serious about their

[13] Sullivan, *Interpersonal Theory of Psychiatry*, p. 227.

disagreements with their elders, for they are among the best educated and informed young people of all time.

From the study of history and from empirical observations of the contemporary life of young people, we may conclude: At the heart of the struggle for growth in adolescence is the struggle for independence. The dramatic, turbulent years of adolescence witness the transition from childhood to adulthood over a relatively brief span of five or six years. Erikson characterizes this epoch as the struggle for ego identity. The adolescent is working out his identity as a person in his own right. However, the task is extremely difficult for him, especially because he remains more or less dependent upon his parents throughout. This dependency-independency conflict is the critical dynamic of adolescent development.

In early adolescence drastic changes in his body initiate the onset of puberty. His body which was once dependable and relatively stable is no longer either. Hormonal activity results in pronounced bodily changes: breast size in girls increases, pubic hair appears, and menstruation begins; the enlargement of testicles, the appearance of pubic hair, and voice changes occur in boys, beginning a few years later than the onset of puberty in girls. Accompanying such obvious changes are the physiological and anatomical concomitants such as the development of primary and secondary sex characteristics, changes in size, weight, bodily proportion, and muscular development and coordination. The boy, for example, just about doubles in muscular development from the age of twelve to seventeen. This rapid spurt of growth over the brief period of time is likely to produce troublesome emotional reaction.

Eventually one of the realities with which the adolescent must deal is that he is now what his biological development has attained. If the boy, for example, who has always aspired to be a great basketball player, finds at sixteen years of age that he is only five feet seven inches tall, the way is exceedingly difficult (although not impossible) for him. This is a limitation he is forced to accept. A fifteen-year-old girl of our acquaintance who has teeth which protrude slightly, a slender body, and a comparatively flat chest, hates her personal appearance and feels doomed to be unattractive for life. However, she is learning to assess her strengths which hopefully will help her to accept what she feels are bodily limitations. She is not even as physically unattractive as she sees herself. Thus, the beginning of the struggle for independence involves the acceptance of one's physical configuration.

Peer Grouping as a Move to Independence

The peer group becomes of critical importance to the adolescent. He transfers his loyalties from the family to significant "in" groups of other young people. The dependency-independency conflict gets focused here. Young people band together for mutual support in their bid for independence. "Here the youth feels accepted because of friendship and finds some respite from judgment and the acceptance on the basis of achievement that is becoming increasingly important in school and to himself as well as his parents." [14] In such groups he can feel more free from parental controls and test out his adult behavior. He can try to act in ways not permitted to him in childhood. Through group support and interaction the adolescent gains new guiding principles for his behavior.

During the so-called period of middle adolescence, movement toward the opposite sex and away from the same sex peer group is taking place. Once the boy and girl become sure of their own sexual identity, which they learn in association and competition with peers of the same sex, they now begin to risk encounters with members of the opposite sex. Usually this begins in "teasing" which is designed to conceal interest while showing it! In order to shore up his feelings of worth about himself, the adolescent strives to develop skills which make him popular.

Experiences of falling in love often occur during middle adolescence. However, the movement toward the person of the opposite sex proceeds rather slowly. Usually the experiences are quite narcissistic, concerned with living out one's fantasies

[14] Lidz, *The Person*, p. 331.

rather than actually engaging the other. However, in the intermingling of the sexes the adolescent's social awareness is expanded. Sexual identity is informed and developed in the interaction which occurs. The boy learns more what a woman is like, and the girl discovers, at least to some degree, the nature of the gap between her fantasies and the reality concerning a man. Therefore, not only does each develop a more realistic notion of the sexual identity of the other, but he gets a better idea of his own.

Fufilling Relationships

"The major tasks of late adolescence concern the achievement of an ego identity and capacities for intimacy" [15] Thus Lidz sums up the central themes of the young person who is emerging from the struggles for independence. He is now faced with the challenge of developing interdependent relationships. I would add to the major tasks the courage of commitment to significant action. The young person enters young adulthood with a passion to be a part of cooperative movements of ultimate significance. The earnest concern to know who he is (ego identity) is not just of psychological significance. but is always in relation to whom, to what, and for what purpose.

In the early years of adolescence withdrawal from the parents has been a painful but normal and necessary process. Psychologically similar to mourning, the phenomenon is often accompanied by feelings of loneliness, isolation, and resentment. Increased desire for self-gratification may result in heightened tendencies toward eating or masturbation. Also, the adolescent turns to adults outside his family for support. He seeks to identify with adults whom he admires and to have guidance from them. "Relationships with adults nevertheless are also perceived as potentially dangerous. This is due to a fear of losing one's individuality and identity." Although the teen-ager wishes to identify with the strengths he perceives in admired adults, he fears being overwhelmed by them. This fear carries

[15] *Ibid.*, p. 342,

over into later adolescence to affect deeply his capacity for intimacy.

Identity Formation

Identity formation, which emerges from the early dependency-independency struggle, does not come just from asking the question, "Who am I?" and expecting answers to flow from some undiscovered reservoir within the self. Identity formation comes from continued encounters with other people, with whose judgments about him he interacts and ultimately assimilates what he learns about himself.[16] Nor is this merely a passive taking-in process; rather, he actively creates an identity which is differentiated out of encounters with people.[17]

For example, in late adolescence the young person is no longer concerned with seeking out and establishing his sexual identity, but with exploring it. Falling in love now involves him in a more intense and genuine concern for his beloved. He is experiencing his developing capacity for genuine affection and tenderness for the other. He is not just driven by sexual feelings. The measure of his maturity is how well he can control rather than be controlled by his feelings. Now, in all regards, he is ready for sexual intimacy. He will also be the decider of whether or not he is ready to assume responsibilities which go along with it. Note the song "I Am Seventeen Going on Eighteen; I Will Take Care of You," from *The Sound of Music*.

Viewing parents and society with a new objectivity, the adolescent becomes aware of failings and hypocrisies of people around him. Answers to perplexing social questions become naïvely clear to him. He sees the Establishment which represents entrenched power as hopelessly enmeshed. His hope is in severing all ties with the "old" culture. In his radical moments

[16] Group for the Advancement of Psychiatry, *Normal Adolescence* (New York: Scribner's, 1968), p. 67.

[17] See Lowell Colson, *Judgment in Pastoral Counseling* (Nashville: Abingdon Press, 1969), especially the chapter "Assimilation of Judgment," pp. 36-53.

or if he listens to revolutionary counterparts, he may feel he must destroy it to be truly free. To justify his need for independence he may caricature the faults of his parents or exaggerate them out of proportion.

Integrating Operations

Integrating tendencies are operating persistently in the young person. He is pulling together data from all sources, including his parents, into a new organization. "Identity formation has much to do with the person's past identifications and their fusion into a new integrate. The identifications with the parents remain basic despite the many vicissitudes they have undergone, but to them have been added the identifications with various ideal figures and both friends and enemies, for something remains of all." [18] The adolescent is reorganizing all he has received from his past and present experiencing into a new identity.

The achievement of ego identity depends in part upon gaining a capacity for intimacy. The adolescent's experiencing of what is meant by loving and being loved enables him to develop trust and find fulfillment in relationships. The youth learns to become less self-centered and self-indulging in his sexual and affectional needs. The welfare of his partner becomes as important to him as his own. He is learning to risk involvement without being swallowed up in the identity of the other. As his own self-identity increases, he is less fearful of being completely "taken over" by the other. Now he can fall in love in a serious fashion, because he is ready to interact and he is involved with the other. He recognizes that mutual fulfillment of needs comes out of responsible relationships.

During late adolescence normally the desire becomes heightened to participate cooperatively in fostering movements of larger significance. Serious concern with ethics, politics, and religion becomes evident. The adolescent is forming new ideals and is shaping his conscience to implement them. He has

[18] Lidz, *The Person*, p. 345.

learned to think in concepts. In fact, if we can generally characterize childhood as the training ground for the development of language and skills in symbolization, we can regard adolescence as a similar time for developing concept formation.

In late adolescence the youth is becoming increasingly discerning of the essential unity of things, while making a critical differentiation of their constituent parts. Ideas can be weighed, measured, and challenged, not merely embraced or rejected. He is able to commit himself to long or dangerous periods of training for a specific task. He comes to regard certain political, social, and religious causes as worthy of giving his life to, or for if necessary. He is now ready to take seriously the preparation for a vocation and marriage, which are pivotal tasks of young adulthood into which he is entering.

He is ready, as Ross Synder suggests, to "participate in the passion and action of our times." He is facing the questions Synder frames: "How do you go about deciding where to situate your life so that things will begin to happen to you? Where will you get awakened? Where your life could cause things to happen and be a part of cumulating consequences?" [19] The adolescent's answers to these questions set the course for his struggles toward growth in young adulthood. What he does about them will affect directly his sense of vocation and his image of himself as a meaningful person.

6. Young Adulthood: Enriching Interdependence

As the young person moves from adolescence into adulthood, he is challenged to engage with others in the diversified activities which will involve him for the remainder of his life. Lidz has well summed up how adolescence prepares him for his task:

1. He has become reasonably independent of his parents.
2. He has achieved an identity, which includes what he has

[19] *Young People and Their Culture* (Nashville: Abingdon Press, 1969), p. 113.

appropriated from other significant persons, even those whom he has sought to reject.

3. The directives which guide him in choosing what are acceptable and unacceptable norms of behavior transcend parental dictates.

4. He has greater self-control, in that he is now able to delay immediate gratifications for the sake of long-range goals for personal fulfillment.

5. He has learned adaptive behavior, which requires the capacity to tolerate tensions, frustrations, and the inevitable anxieties of life and still adhere to objectives and work through difficulties.

6. Frustrations are recognized as a part of life. They are avoided if possible, but accepted when necessary "without mobilizing undue hostility and aggression." Whatever aggression is aroused is directed toward tackling the problem rather than attacking others or one's self in vengeance.

7. The boundaries of the self are sufficiently secure to forestall the fear of unconsciously losing one's identity when he strives for intimacy.

8. The person is secure enough in his sexual identity not to be forced compulsively to prove his masculinity or femininity by repetitive sexual activity. Nor does the youth need to assure himself or others of that identity by compulsive acts of masculine aggression or feminine seductiveness.[20]

The whole of the foregoing represents a large order for the young person, but indicates an optimal level of preparation for the interdependence of young adulthood.

"His independence from his natal family requires that he achieve an interdependence with others and find his place in the social system. Through vocation and marriage he is united to networks of persons, finds tasks that demand involvement, and gains roles into which he fits and is fitted which help define his identity." [21]

[20] Lidz, The Person, pp. 364-67.
[21] Ibid., p. 363.

Freedom to "do his own thing" and "to be his own man" continues to be important, but now the young person must take account of others, upon whom he depends to some degree and who depend upon him. He learns to negotiate his differences with them. He discovers he must give up certain prerogatives, while others are opening to him.

For the young person the choice of an occupation sets up a whole new way of life. It is not just a way of earning a living, or learning skills and functions. He is now faced with the prospect of becoming involved in a network of relationships to which he contributes himself. He influences and is influenced by the people with whom he works. Thus, his occupation plays a significant role in determining his values and his ethical judgments. He often adapts himself to the expectations of his occupational group, and may even seek to hold together conflicting values of groups which are important to him. This is especially true of the man, if he is the breadwinner of the family, but also applies, to a corresponding degree, to the woman affected by the occupational choice of her husband.

A new language and culture develops for both of them. For example, a young woman of my acquaintance married a driver of racing cars who travels around the country competing in races. She has entered a society which has its own language and culture. Although the people, in their talk and interests, are strange to her, she is struggling to understand and become a part of them. Whether a couple be involved in auto racing, in the business community, in a profession, or whatever, they enter a unique culture.

Marriage is also an event requiring the development of interdependence. A shift in personal organization is necessary from that centered around one's own interests and concerns to include those of the partner. A new social system is created. The previous patterns of ethical and social behavior, which undoubtedly differ, more or less, between marriage partners, must be reworked into a new family system. A satisfying and completing interpersonal relationship is requisite to all else. Mutual sexual fulfillment, parenthood, and other activities of the family are based upon it.

Nevertheless, even the best-matched couples encounter difficulties in adjusting to each other. If they can successfully negotiate their differences, they set in motion a process by which they learn to live together. They create new patterns of relating and establish new values. The marriage partners tend to complement each other and live together harmoniously in a wide variety of ways. No dependable "given pathway" can be assumed. Each couple works out ways of relating which bring a measure of satisfaction to each spouse.

As Erikson has aptly put it, "Intimate love thus is the guardian of that elusive and yet all-pervasive power in psychosocial evolution: The power of *cultural and personal style*, which gives and demands conviction in the shared patterns of living, guarantees individual identity in joint intimacy, and binds into a 'way of life' the affiliations of procreation and production." [22]

Interdependence is not a weakening of self-identity; on the contrary, it is a strengthening of one's identity. Certainly a creative marriage is the product of the interaction between spouses who are sufficiently interdependent and integrating in their relationship to live interdependently. They will not seek just to be harmonious, but to be working creatively to bring novelty, freshness, and originality into their marriage. Thus they will be continually renewing their relationship and strengthening the family which they create.

Increasing Responsibility

The assumption of an occupation and the initiating of a marriage relationship implies increased responsibility. The young adult no longer has merely or primarily concern for his own welfare. What he does on his job affects perhaps scores of other people. In marriage the welfare of the spouse now

[22] *Insight and Responsibility* (New York: W. W. Norton, 1964), p. 128.

becomes, in some measure, the responsibility of the other spouse.

Furthermore, the coming of children introduces a switch in roles. The responsibilities of parenthood have become real. Whereas even in young adulthood the young couple see themselves as children of their parents, now they are parents of their own children.

The reality of the new role comes to the woman during her pregnancy when, as she becomes aware of the fetal life within her, she concentrates upon the preparation for motherhood. She may turn much of her attention and emotional investment to the newborn child. The husband may not get the full impact of his parental role until much later. In fact, he may actually feel forced out of the affectional interdependency he had presumed to have established with his wife. In this sense he may feel threatened by and even resentful of the newborn child. However, as he interacts with his wife in the process of receiving the newcomer into his own emotional life, and as the relationship between them is strengthened by mutual supportiveness, the newly developing family is nurtured and stabilized.

Beyond his family, furthermore, is his growing responsibility for the world around him. As he sees what needs his love and concern, he takes the issue upon himself. Drawing upon his experiencing of creative unity in his occupation and marriage, he devotes himself to "subduing the antagonism inherent in divided functions" [23] of people and groups with whom he lives.

He may do this in blind devotion to the ideals he espouses. If so, such is not true responsibility. He is called to engage in dialogue with those who disagree with him, and becomes discerning as to how to deal with the antagonisms. He may resolve to act courageously in the face of what he perceives as self-interested criticism on the part of his adversaries. Or he may be sufficiently persuasive to enlist cooperative effort to unite.

[23] *Ibid*, p. 129.

7. *Middle Adulthood: Fulfilling Responsibility*

Extending Care and Compassion

For some, the middle years are considered a time of fulfillment and realization. Years of effort and struggle are being rewarded with fruition. For others, middle life is met in bitterness and disappointment. For all, a recognition that time has passed, and many an opportunity with it, activates existential anxiety. An awareness of the limits of available time becomes acute. Realizing, also, that the body is gradually slowing down, the man or woman may begin to reevaluate himself. Writers have characterized the middle years in various ways. Smiley Blanton speaks of *Now or Never*, Reuel Howe writes of *The Creative Years*, Carl Jung regards the middle life as the time of "spiritual maturity." Most writers see this epoch as a period of heavy responsibility and heightened creativity.

Fortunately, man has a vested interest in what he produces, whether by design or by accident. He is concerned to see what he has brought into being grow and flourish. The interest he has is not just response to an obligation. His care for what is generated from him—whether his works or his children—brings him personal fulfillment. They verify his selfhood. He needs to be needed.

The field in which the authors of this book work is often designated as "pastoral care." In the context of the ministry, care means concern for the growth and welfare of the people of the Christian community. This activity is analogous to the preoccupation of those in the middle years who seek to transmit "the rudiments of hope, will, purpose, and competence" to their children as well as to stimulate the creation of a life style and a world view by them.

Compassion is the appropriate attitude for caring. Compassion is not to be interpreted as pitying suffering people, or engaging in naïve sentimentality in regard to them. Rather compassion is truly entering imaginatively into the other person's suffering, even if the suffering is largely of the latter's own making. He may then be encouraged to face up to others

126

or to himself and appropriate his suffering as a means to growth, rather than excusing himself through self-pity. "Arise, take up your bed and walk" was neither the expression of a self-styled faith healer nor the command of a calloused cynic, but the calm, confident challenge of a compassionate soul.

When one can be said to be truly compassionate he has reached the heights of maturity! He is able to enter into the experiences with others and *feel* with them. Yet he is not fearful of those feelings; therefore he can be helpful. To be compassionate is to be with the other person and participate in a communion that cannot be disturbed. The compassionate can be deeply sensitive to the other person, yet not manipulated by him.

Maintaining Fidelity

During middle life some persons may try to salvage their lives by making radical changes. They may try to change spouses or jobs. These are years which may put the marriage to a critical test. When the children have left the natal home, the parents are left to face each other. They may have been so diverted and preoccupied with the children that they are not really prepared for that event. Divorces and remarriages often occur at that time. Many times the spouses select partners strikingly similar to those they have abandoned.

A change in jobs may be regarded as the key to renewal of life. Although "retooling" for a new vocation may be impracticable if not virtually impossible, a change in position may be sought for the ego enhancement desired. Thus the middle-aged man, for example, struggles to maintain his dignity as a man.

The middle-age crisis of women in regard to ego identity is more specific than in men. "Many women have a very focused identity during their first forty years: They are the creators and sustainers of life." [24] Very obvious changes occur in the woman which affect this identity. Her ovaries atrophy, menstruation ceases, her capacity for ovulation ceases and with it

[24] James A. Peterson, *Married Love in the Middle Years*, (New York: Association Press, 1968), p. 72.

the possibility for motherhood. She now faces the task of resolving the resulting identity crisis.

The woman in her middle years will undoubtedly find the solution to her identity crisis in a richer relationship with her husband. If she can understand and be aware of his identity needs at this time, she will not always be frustrated when he does not respond to her needs. However, since the woman has largely assumed the expressive function, she may switch the concentration of her love for her children to him.

The central focus of the man's identity crisis is the need to find meaning in his life. The answer to this is contained in the term "fidelity." He needs to keep faith with himself and with those whom he loves, as well as with his friends. Fidelity is the capacity to sustain loyalties to commitments made, regardless of the inevitable contradictions in life, He should do an inventory of the previous years and count the cost of achievements he has made. Rather than brood about the lost years, he will do well to acknowledge with gratitude the wisdom he has gained from the experiences he has had.

Beyond fidelity to friends, family, and the community in faithful service is the person's religious faith. The middle years are potentially most creative in this regard. "Complaining to God about fate and asking for some divine manipulation to ease the paradox of life produces little but disillusionment with faith. The curious and creative searcher is rarely a cynic." [25] The man who is earnestly engaging in searching and dialogue recognizes that he is only on the edge of truth and "more truth is yet to be revealed." Nevertheless, he finds vitality, renewal, and hope in his dialogue with the great religious thinkers of the past and with contemporary theologians who stimulate his thought about the meaning of existence. His involved faith and commitment bring great rewards in the achievement of perspective upon his life and reality.

In the face of the tremendous uncertainties, perplexing ambiguities, and often frightening irrationalities of the times in which we live, this loyal focus on the theological enterprise

[25] *Ibid*, p. 122.

is highly essential. Actually the power of such profound inter-action—not a kind of uneasy, anxious, superficial backslapping in which we try pathetically and absurdly to reassure ourselves and others—is the dynamic to spur on faith in God's con-tinuing redeeming activity in the world.

8. Older Maturity: Expanding the Spirit

The central task of older age is that of dignified *disengagement* from the active arenas of life. Problems which arise from retirement, facing the end of life, and declining physical and mental powers combine to make this phase of the life cycle a difficult one for the older persons in our society. The difficulty in this disengagement process largely arises out of the conflict in feeling in the older person over whether or not the dis-engaging is by his decision or is forced upon him. In the former he feels he is freeing himself from heavy demands and respon-sibilities and choosing the conditions of his contrived involve-ment. In the latter he feels pushed out, unwanted, having out-lived his usefulness.

Old age has been rather arbitrarily set at age sixty-five, when most employers set retirement for their employees. Increasingly, many do not feel that they are "elderly." In fact, they did not feel essentially different from the way they functioned in their middle years. They are capable, productive, and competent to take care of themselves and to contribute in many ways to society.

Therefore, I (LGC) consider the primary tasks of older maturity those of *stimulating creativity* and *fostering com-munity*. These tasks are the outgrowth of what Erikson calls the primary virtue of older maturity—*wisdom*. "Strength in the old," Erikson says, "takes the form of wisdom in all of its connotations from ripened wits to accumulated knowledge free from temporal relativity. *Wisdom, then, is detached con-cern with life itself, in the face of death itself.*" [26] Such wis-dom is the spark of creativity and gives integrity to community life.

[26] Erikson, *Insight and Responsibility*, p. 133.

Realizing Creativity

Contrary to many popular notions, older maturity is still a time of growth, when the experience and wisdom which has been accumulated is employed to pull things together. It is a time of potential creativity. The retired person is freed from the narrowing demands of a particular job in a particular place. The routine of making a living while working at a specific task is broken. He may now put his energies and abilities where he wishes. He may thus be enabled to gain a perspective upon life heretofore shut off by his limited preoccupation with earning a livelihood. Of course, he may not do things either. He may not have the assets and resources of a few gifted who have become even more productive in their older age.

The familiar stories of Grandma Moses, Frank Lloyd Wright, Picasso, and others among the creative artists have become almost legendary. Political leaders and jurists such as Winston Churchill and Chief Justice Holmes have been among those who seemed to mellow with aging. Although many are probably less gifted, the examples of even these few show the possibilities open to older people who are willing to experience life actively and to maintain their vital concerns into old age. This fact argues eloquently for a person's involvement in continued education throughout his life to open up numerous avenues of interest and activity.

Older maturity does not have to be a time of disengagement leading to despair. Medical science has improved aids to physical impairments which may develop to the point of remarkable technical efficiency. Furthermore, writers like Alvin Goldfarb insist that "people who are motivated toward self-realization" and who "believe that youthful interests and vigor can continue into the later years" do not need to retreat because they are aging.[27] We do not accept the assertion that the older person is beyond creativity. However, we urge young people and those in middle years to be concerned to develop a way of life which

[27] Alvin I. Goldfarb in the Foreword to Isadore Rubin, *Sexual Life After Sixty* (New York: Basic Books, 1965), p. vii.

releases their creative potential throughout the years of their
development. In this way they will be equipped to realize the
creative potential of their older maturity. And the open or
closed attitude of younger persons toward older persons brings
them impetus to fruition or decline.

Maintaining Community

The person of older maturity can, and often does, give integrity to the community of which he is a part. He may serve
as the symbol of unity to the family and the community. Also
he may be a hopeful and promising model for identification of
children and grandchildren and a tie to preceding generations,
which give his family a sense of history and meaning.

Michael Smart was such a person. Some of my most pleasant
early memories were of associations with Mr. Smart and his
large family of children, in-laws, and grandchildren who met,
at least annually, for a grand reunion. It seems to me to be
about the most exciting and interesting get-together of one
family I had ever experienced.

"Micky" Smart, as he was known to his many friends, lived
on a southern Iowa farm which had provided the livelihood
for eight children. He was the "head" of the family, who in his
old age became a rallying point, the symbol of the family's
life and character. He was not a patriarch in the negative sense
of a witting or unwitting tyrant, but a kind, beneficent man
of high purpose and great spirit whose acceptance of his
children earned him the respect they showed.

I (LGC) saw him not many years before his death, in the
little country church in which he had worshiped for many
years. No one could doubt the high esteem in which he was
held by his neighbors and fellow townspeople. His presence in
their midst was conspicuous by the positive regard they had
for him and his family. He symbolized honesty, industry, integrity, responsibility, and patient love. His very presence welded
the community together into a harmonious fellowship. He was
calm and respectful in expressing his differences with his fel-
lows. Yet, this was not a subtle way of forcing his will on them,

He was open to their arguments and supportive of their causes when they seemed just and fair. He was admired and respected because on many occasions he demonstrated his humanity and acknowledged his common bond to his friends. He gave integrity to the community.

The wisdom of older maturity serves integrity, if the older person will draw upon it, and if younger leaders of the community will accept it. The latter argue that in a rapidly changing society the wisdom of the past is not needed. Therefore, they conclude, older people tend to impede or block progress through their reactionary conservatism. Nevertheless, ways of drawing upon this wisdom and the potential creativity of older persons should be devised. Social systems which simply provide custodial care and create dependencies among the older persons are an affront to those persons and a waste of their real potential. Self-esteem requires at least some degree of genuine self-sufficiency. Perhaps through the tendency to "sideline" older persons we sacrifice integrity of the community for the doubtful one-dimensional value of progress.

The life cycle concludes in death, which has been the subject of a number of recent treatises concerned to see how the inevitability of death affects man's life. We shall not deal with that aspect of the life cycle, since our main concern has been to discuss themes in the struggle for growth. Yet growth is also needed in the face of death.

We have highlighted: the psychobiological development of the child—his discovery of himself and his differentiation of himself from the world; the psychosocial development of the juvenile—his discovery of others and his learning of basic patterns of relating and organizing; the psychosexual development of the adolescent (which began in infancy)—his discovery of the sexual nature of the person of the opposite sex, his resolving of the dependency-independency conflict, and his learning to develop his capacity for intimacy. We observed the struggle of the young adult for identity and his learning to achieve the interdependence required for occupational and marital fulfillment. We have noted the needs of middle-aged persons to develop their capacities for care, compassion, and fidelity. Finally we have emphasized the creative contributions and potential of older persons, acknowledging the strength and integrity their accrued wisdom gives to the community.

Although we have recognized themes which we consider appropriate to each stage in the life cycle, we have not put them in a strictly deterministic framework. We say that decision is the action which expands personal consciousness. Responsible decision-making is the mark of a growing person.

We conclude that the self-actualizing person is increasingly sensitive and responsible. He is deeply aware of others, because he opens himself to them. He decides and accepts responsibility for the consequences of his decision. He understands the problems of people in a particular developmental period, because he is open to what they are experiencing.

Now that we have viewed the expanding personal consciousness, psychologically and socially, how do we view this phenomenon theologically? Such is the concern of the concluding part of this book.

Three: Consciousness and Faith

VII

Anguishing Dilemmas of Growth

We believe that Christian faith is especially relevant to the contemporary revolution in personal consciousness, and vice versa. In fact, we see antecedents of it in the early Christian community. Experiences at Pentecost are notable examples of the impact of faith on personal spirit. Some religious groups have distorted the meaning of those experiences by concentrating on one aspect of the total phenomenon. They have played up what God does and played down the character of human responsiveness. Thus, although they are aware of the nonintellective dimensions of personal consciousness, they come out anti-intellectual in their approach. This is as one-sided as the distortions they seek to overcome.

As we pointed out in the introduction to this book, the Christian community is by intention a liberating and facilitating community. The person is freed to love deeply and responsibly. Thus he is stimulated to grow in his appreciation of others and the world. This is not automatic by any means. The seeming paradox of receiving by giving is not always understood or acted upon. We often feel we must control ourselves and others in order to be safe.

A person's faith reflects his fundamental view of the world. His basic position or stance in life is influenced by that faith. If he believes that existence is a dirty trick and death an absurdity, he lives in accord with that belief. As he gains perspective upon life and the world, he acts in terms of it. He is thus opened up to his own possibilities.

The opening up is a response of love and giving. If he is truly opened to the essence of the thing or person to whom he is relating, he will become more aware of the creative activity of God in the world. At the same time he becomes more responsible for what he does with that important knowledge. This is one of the anguishing dilemmas of growth: whether to close oneself off from the pain and suffering of others—hopefully not to hurt so much in ourselves—or to open up and bear the pain and responsibility of loving others, and to become potentially a greater servant of all! How does Christian faith help us to deal with such anguishing dilemmas in our growth?

Human life is actually too complex for simple answers. In one sense growth is inevitable and irresistible. Witness the tiny root splitting the rock by the steady expanding power of its growth. And yet plants die if the soil and atmosphere are not sufficient to nourish growth. The astronauts found no trace of life on the moon because the environment does not provide the complex richness to sustain growing life. A Harvard scientist has shown that 214 environmental conditions have to be present in accurate proportion for the simplest life to exist on our planet.[1] And moving to human life, we find the conditions of growth infinitely more complex in ever-changing and interacting interrelationships.

We have therefore sought to trace the psychosocial interactions of persons in their struggles for creative growth. We have focused on the crises and developmental tasks in each stage of our upward journey from infancy and childhood, adolescence and young adulthood, to mid-life and older maturity. We have seen how far human life reaches out by enlarging participation in our world of persons and society through the sharing of values and individual differences in community.

Now we turn the searchlight inward to know ourselves more deeply. How do we feel in the depths of our being as we struggle to grow? Growing is an endless series of tasks in every

[1] Many more conditions are being discovered as science progresses.

age from birth to death. There are autonomic processes constantly at work to innervate the smooth and cardiac muscles and glandular tissues that govern the circulation of fluids to nourish the whole organism. Yet this even flow of life can be disturbed by emotions and events in relation to other persons in our world. We are psychosomatic social beings interdependent and interacting in dynamic systems within and among persons. What adventures beset and challenge us on the inward journey of life?

Karl Menninger on the advancing frontier of modern psychiatry offers a useful model for understanding human behavior which he calls *the vital balance.*[2] The human organism is seen as a living system interacting with other systems. The individual organism is interacting and mutually adapting to the changing stimuli and systems of the environment. While at the same time within the organism are many psychobiochemical processes interacting and mutually adjusting in dynamic processes. When all these outer-inner processes are in vital balance, we enjoy health and fulfillment.

But when this vital balance is disturbed by stress from without or within the organism, there are minor or major crises to accommodate and work through to a new balance. In this organismic "system theory," a regulating process is constantly at work within the growing person to bring stresses into a steady state of equilibrium to maintain one's unique integrity. The regulator of these dynamic processes is known as the ego, mediating the pressures and guiding the responses to achieve a working balance. Otherwise life is distorted, blocked, conflicted, and reduced to less effective behavior.

The anguishing dilemmas which concern us in this chapter arise in the need to maintain a wholesome vital balance in the midst of the inner-outer stresses of a growing person. No one can hope to be safe at all times in all ways. Stresses arise from hour to hour to disturb the ever-changing balance and call for conscious and unconscious adjustment. It has been wryly

[2] *The Vital Balance: The Life Process in Mental Health* (New York: Viking Press, 1963).

139

said, there are so many dangers between the cradle and the grave, it's a wonder we ever reach the grave. Each day we grow a little and die a little, we learn something and forget more, as we meet the impacting pressures of life by adjusting this way or that.

1. Anxiety or Trust

Anxiety is close to the center of every person. Who can live without anxiety? This is a universal experience we all share in our common life. Anxiety is causing us anguish not easy to bear, until we sometimes feel we would do almost anything to be rid of it. Yet anxiety serves a useful purpose, and when it is properly heeded it brings important messages we do well to accept and understand. What is the nature and purpose of anxiety?

Freud gives a clinical view of anxiety as an alarm system to signal the presence of danger which alerts us to respond. "Anxiety is a reaction to a situation of danger." [3] Anxious feelings occur at birth, and in the infantile experiences of separation from the mother's breast, or being alone in the dark, or fear of punishment, withdrawal of protective support, and other acute losses. Anxiety differs from other forms of pain by its tendency to act and discharge in particular paths. A sharp awareness of need mingles with a feeling of helplessness and a desire to avoid, correct, or restore the well being.

Yet anxiety does not tell us how to respond to a sense of danger. There are various reactions such as crying, frustration, angry fighting, withdrawing, seeking to recover what is lost, or symptoms of bodily and emotional adjustment to the stress. This is more than reflex action or physiological reaction, as Freud came in his later years to see very well. At first he had held that anxiety arose automatically. But in 1923 he wrote: "The ego is the actual seat of anxiety." [4] It is only the ego

[3] *Inhibitions, Symptoms and Anxiety* (1925), in *The Complete Psychological Works of Sigmund Freud*, Standard Edition, Vol. XX (London: Hogarth Press, 1959), p. 128.
[4] *The Ego and the Id*, Standard Edition, Vol. XIX, p. 57.

which is organized to make a judgment about situations of danger.[5] And when the ego recognizes danger either from without or within, the ego will decide how to cope with the danger.

Animals react automatically in fear to a stimulus of danger. They may discharge energy by flight or fight in frenzied motion. Or they may cower in tense and frozen immobility. A growing person is responsive to a wider range of more subtle dangers. And he holds the stress within himself as he considers what it means and how to respond. In the complexity and continuity of human experience anxiety may become a chronic endless state, an unresolved load to bear.

When John was six years old his parents noticed some irregularities in his speech. This disturbed them, and impelled by their anxiety they began to correct him.

"John, you are stuttering," they said. "Speak more slowly."

So their anxiety was communicated to John, and reinforced by constant reminders that his speech was disturbing them. He felt something was wrong with him, that his spontaneous way of speaking was not accepted by others.

"Stop now, and think what you are going to say," his father would respond whenever John started to speak. The father was a preacher and valued public speaking as a fine art, demanding clear diction and fluent speech.

"Let me help you," the father would say. "Speak like this," he would demonstrate in measured exact syllables.

John wanted to please, and the more he was corrected the more anxious he would become. While before he spoke freely and hopefully to others whatever came to mind, now he hesitated to speak lest he be corrected. He became tense, cautious and guarded, fearing that he might offend others by speaking out naturally.

His mother and brother Ed, (sixteen months older), reflected the family anxiety too, and tried to help him in their way by prompting him. When John would begin a sentence and hesi-

[5] See *Inhibitions, Symptoms and Anxiety*, p. 140.

141

tate, they would complete the sentence for him. This showed him how to do it, and also how they could speak better than he. Rather than improving his speech, these family efforts only helped him to stutter more painfully. When he tried to say a word his vocal muscles cramped and stopped the sound from coming out. So he was caught in a bind with his mouth open, struggling helplessly to speak. This caused other persons to stare at him in astonishment and distress until he was so ashamed he felt inferior and painfully self-conscious.

What would you do in this anguishing dilemma if you were six years old? You could not escape home or talk it out in open communication. The usual alternative when communication is blocked is to act out your feelings. John's feelings of anxiety, stress, inferiority, and shame were not simple but quite complex. He acted them out in various ways:

1. He was *submissive and obedient* in trying to do what his father said. But the more he tried to please his father by speaking "right," the more tense, anxious, and caught he was in his stuttering. Exerting more effort only tightened the knot of his vocal spasms and sharpened his sense of shame and failure.

2. He sought *love* from his mother by "mixing up kisses," bringing them to her, and snuggling closer to her. She was kind and loving, so he felt comforted when he was with her.

3. He was *angry* with his brother, and after school one day snatched Ed's prized marble shooter from the ring and ran. Ed chased him all the way home, jumped on him and pounded him with his fists. When the father came home and learned of the fight, he placed the brothers in separate bedrooms where he talked with each brother, listening to each story, and asking what to do next.

4. He tried to *repress* his anxiety when the physician advised his parents to "pay no attention to his stuttering and it will go away."

Anxiety is a signal of danger to the vital balance of life. If the danger passes, we may expect the anxiety to vanish. But if the danger remains, our anxiety becomes a chronic state of "dis-ease." Tensions may cripple freedom in many ways. Breathing and circulation are constricted, chemical balance upset, and creativity reduced by cautious withdrawal. Many seek escape in alcohol, drugs, tranquilizers, television, travel, changing jobs or mates, and moving away. If we focus on escape we then devote our energies to flight in getting lost, or discharge anxiety in reckless impulsive behavior.

What shall we do with anxiety? Human life can never be free of anxiety, and if it were, who would want such an empty vegetable existence? When lobotomy of the forebrain has been used as a surgical procedure to relieve excessive anxiety, the result has been an aimless, incompetent, meaningless vacuum. If we agree that we will have to live with anxiety, the question is how to make the most of each challenge in whatever situations we face.

Yet if we plumb more deeply the stream of our growing experience, we may find an inner resource to dissolve anxiety. This resource is known as *trust*. The experience of trust is well known as one of the most profound influences of a religious life. The psychologist Erikson says, "We have learned to regard basic trust as the cornerstone of a healthy personality." [6]

The foundation of trust, as we have seen, is formed in the first year of life through the quality of the relationship to the mother. To give this trusting quality to a child, the mother must have a deep conviction that there is meaning to what they are doing. If she gives sensitive care to the baby's needs and conveys a sense of trustworthiness, she undergirds the child with a trusting world.

This infant paradise, however, cannot last forever. All too soon the mother will have to withdraw, and there is a rift in the wholeness of life. So the child learns to mistrust and comes to know the pain of separation and loss. If the mother is displeased or angry, the baby feels a loss of love; and closeness to the mother is no longer comforting but anxious. From these various experiences the growing person moves between

[6] *Identity and the Life Cycle*, p. 56.

trust and mistrust until he develops a ground pattern of expectancies.

As he teeters between the upswing of love and the downswing of loss, the growing child will settle into a more prevailing mood which becomes the undertone of his life. This is the first major crisis in his psychosocial growth. Will he lean toward basic mistrust as his dominant mood? If so, new experiences will tend to confirm this expectancy that persons are not to be trusted and life is fraught with danger and distress. He may be so depressed that he is not aroused by signs of hope, but withdraws in despair like the autistic child.

If on the other hand the growing person has strong reinforcing experiences of love and trustworthiness, he is more able to rest his expectations in basic trust. He will of course meet his share of disappointments and defeats; he will face dangers and know anxiety on his life journey. But if he has well learned the lessons of basic trust, he will have ego strength to cope with the shocks and losses when they come; he will have inner resources and courage to live through the changing scenes of life with all their dangers and difficulties.

This is more than a question of individual temperament, for each person is open to his world and sensitive to the moods and behavior of others. Each person lives in a context of interpersonal relations, susceptible to social influences as he interacts with others in the many transactions of daily life. He emerges into wholeness only as he can experience a wholeness in community with other persons who participate together in a whole world.

There is no question, as Erikson shows, that organized religion is a powerful force for wholeness.[7] When the family is related to a loving and trusting religious community, these attitudes are reinforced by participation in a group manifesting this way of life. Parents are more able to be at peace within themselves and give loving and trusting responses to growing children. When a family is accustomed to confess their mis-

[7] *Identity: Youth and Crisis* (New York: W. W. Norton 1968), p. 83.

takes and forgive each other, the blocks and resistances may be dissolved and tensions more readily removed. Prayer affirms the goodness of life in spite of distress and sorrow, with continuing aspiration and trusting devotion to share and create a better life.

At its root anxiety is the fear of being abandoned—of being without hope. Thus, a corollary of anxiety is despair. If one seems trapped or helpless in his situation, he experiences high anxiety. Hence, if he cannot truly trust anyone, the person's anxiety becomes intolerable. By the same token, the development of his capacity to trust diminishes his anxiety. Faith generates the capacity for deep trust.

2. Guilt or Acceptance

If separation from the mother is the first breach in the wholeness of life, this is not all. Another crisis comes to the growing person when the parents disapprove his behavior. He may be spanked or ignored to punish him for crying. In toilet training he will be scolded for not obeying the rules. When he spills the cup of milk or breaks something, his parents may be angry and let him feel rejected and unloved. Within himself he comes to feel a split between the "good me" who is approved and the "bad me" who is disapproved.

In this anguishing dilemma the growing person is developing a conscience. As Freud shows, this inner conflict is essential to the formation of character. As the child identifies with his parents and both fears and admires them, so he comes to introject their moral authority into himself as his superego. They become his model or ego ideal. In this way he is able to judge himself by moral standards that become his own conscience. And if the parents do not punish the "bad me," he will punish himself in feeling guilty as unworthy to be approved.

Parental influence governs the child by offering proofs of love and by threatening punishments which are signs to the child of loss of love and are bound to be feared on their own account. This realistic anxiety is the precursor of the later moral anxiety (*Gewissensangst*, literally "conscience anxiety"). . . . The external restraint is internalized and the superego takes the place of the parental agency and observes, directs, and threatens the ego in exactly the same way as earlier the parents did with the child.[8]

In this way the ego becomes responsible to his conscience as his own inner authority. And just as a social person will look to see others respond with approval or disapproval, so the moral person is concerned to meet the inner standards of his own conscience. He suffers more guilt in disobeying his conscience than in disobeying external authorities. He may turn his back on others, but he cannot escape the inner judge who is ever present and causes him the painful anguish of guilt. Martin Luther called this the worst of all ills, "that the conscience cannot run away from itself." [9]

We may see the shaping of this inner authority of conscience in little John as he interacted with his family. At first he had no anxiety about his irregular speech. But when his father said, "You are stuttering," and persisted in correcting him, he felt that he was disapproved for not speaking right. When he tried to speak correctly, he wanted to please his father as the external authority. Yet every correction from his family caused him to feel the shame and guilt of their disapproval. As the tension of such anxiety mounted, he was unable to speak fluently, and the harder he tried the more helpless he was to remove the block to speaking forth freely.

Now he came to monitor his own speech in a self-conscious anxiety. Even when his family did not correct him, he said to himself, "I must not stutter." Feeling guilty about his speech, he was not so free and spontaneous, but anxious in the presence of his elders, fearing that he could not win their approval. The impulse to blurt out his feelings and ideas in open communication was checked by the fear that he would stutter and suffer anew the anguish of shame and disapproval.

[8] *New Introductory Lectures on Psychoanalysis* (1933), Standard Edition, Vol. XXII, p. 62.
[9] Erik Erikson, *Young Man Luther* (New York: W. W. Norton, 1958), p. 258.

Yet in all this there was a deeper sense of unity as one family standing by and caring for each other in every need, of searching for true moral standards to uphold together for the best of each and all. When conflicts arose within the family, each member was to be his own judge in family council. Through such times of self-examination and interchange each person was invited to be an authority in his own right, and take the responsibility to decide what is right and wrong in these events. The external authority of the parents was becoming the inner authority of the boys to wrestle with guilt and decide what to do in the future.

How well did the boys learn these lessons of trustworthy inner authority? Not perfectly or once for all, but little by little, by living as a family, acting out their feelings, making their mistakes, talking them over, and inviting each one to consider and decide right from wrong as the basis for guilt and reparation. No one abdicated authority to others, yet each was aware of a higher authority. They were a Christian family who read the Bible to learn the Ten Commandments, the Golden Rule of doing unto others as you would have them do to you, to love one another as God loves, to pray for guiding wisdom and courage to follow the way of justice, forgiveness, and unselfish service. A sense of guilt is not entirely negative, for it has a positive thrust to reach higher norms and fulfill greater potentials of growth and achievement.

It is evident to family counselors that without a forgiving spirit, conflicts can never be healed, but set into cold resentment that may resist all efforts toward reconciliation. There are many sides to the interpersonal sense of guilt and acceptance. When two persons are related in a situation of conflict, each one may hold the other guilty. The husband may blame the wife, and the wife may blame the husband, neither one accepting the blame for their conflict. Through counseling they may come to see that each one is causing hurt in the other, and therefore each one will need to acknowledge his responsibility for the marital stress. If they can work this out through mutual forgiveness and responsibility to change, they may achieve a better marriage. But if the husband has an affair, the wife may not be willing or able to forgive, and they are blocked with no reconciling love to make a new start. Or if the wife is willing to forgive, but the husband cannot forgive himself, the barrier remains.

Family patterns may involve the entire family in a dynamic tangle of interlocking conflicts which Sherrill describes as malignant relationships, where persons are locked together in a prison of interacting anxiety, hostility, and guilt.[10] Disapproval in hostility induces anxiety, while the pain of anxiety induces hostility, causing and caused by guilt. This vicious circle is so confining and endlessly repetitive that escape is extremely difficult. To cure this accentuating dilemma we need to change the pathological relations into therapeutic relationships by introducing a new and ever-forgiving love. Such love is the New Testament *agape*, which is divinely faithful and self-giving love to heal the self-seeking and fatal alienation of human conflict.

Menninger quotes a newspaper clipping with the headline "Father on Trial in Fatal Belt Beating of Six-Year-Old Son." [11] The pathologist testified the boy died as the result of repeated blows; there were at least ninety-three abrasions on the child's body, he said. The District Attorney was seeking a second-degree murder verdict with a maximum penalty of ten to twenty years in prison. The father testified that he beat the boy with a belt for refusing to tell him where he had hidden a toy hammer.

"I told Jackie a father sometimes has to do things to their children they do not like."

After the beating he put his son to bed and massaged his wounds with vaseline.

"Jackie told me, 'I still love you, Daddy.' Those were the last words my son said to me."

In such a situation a father would have great difficulty in forgiving himself. The feeling of guilt would be a very heavy

[10] Lewis J. Sherrill, *Guilt and Redemption* (rev. ed.; Richmond: John Knox Press, 1957).
[11] *The Vital Balance*, p. 217.

burden to bear, unless he could find it possible eventually to accept himself again. Little Jackie was forgiving his father when in his last words he said, "I still love you, Daddy." And this might make it even more difficult for the father to forgive himself. If he were judged guilty by the court and sentenced to ten or twenty years in prison, his anguish of guilt would be intensified by the public condemnation and reinforced by years of being locked in a cell to look at himself and examine his conscience. He would surely need a chaplain or counselor with whom to talk it out, to experience a cleansing catharsis, seeking forgiveness not only from his family but also from society and the ultimate authority of God.

Tillich deals with the healing of anxiety and guilt in terms of "the courage to accept acceptance." [12] Every person is responsible to answer for what he has made of himself. He is his own judge standing over against himself. If he cannot affirm himself, he is enveloped in a cloud of despair, and all life is a struggle to avoid despair. Our conscience is the call to be ourselves. We must have the courage to face our own guilt and wrestle with it until "thou bless me" (Gen. 32:26).

Christianity may be resented and rejected for sharpening the sense of sin and deepening the pain of guilt. Yet a way is always open to return by confession and forgiving love again and again into the wholeness of a new life. Whenever guilt completes its forward thrust, the anguish of feeling condemned may be healed in the love of a new acceptance. Being accepted does not deny the guilt. The courage of confidence takes the guilt into oneself in spite of the pain, to live in penitence and accept a new fulfillment.

The divine self-affirmation is the power that makes self-affirmation of the finite being, the courage to be, possible. Only because being-itself has the character of self-affirmation in spite of nonbeing is courage possible. . . .
Every act of courage is a manifestation of the ground of being.
. . . Not arguments but the courage to be reveals the true nature

[12] *The Courage to Be* (New Haven: Yale University Press, 1952), pp. 163-71.

of being-itself. By affirming our being we participate in the self-affirmation of being-itself. There are no valid arguments for the "existence" of God, but there are acts of courage in which we affirm the power of being, whether we know it or not. If we know it, we accept the acceptance consciously. If we do not know it, we nevertheless accept it and participate in it. And in our acceptance of that which we do not know, the power of being is manifest in us. Courage has revealing power, the courage to be is the key to being itself.[13]

3. Security or Freedom

Security appears to be the first and original desire of life. Within the womb the unborn fetus has every need instantly and constantly met. So perfect does this close-fitting environment seem that the newborn will naturally miss it and long to return to the womb. Expulsion at birth into the larger world may well be the traumatic crisis whose imprint is not entirely lost, as Rank insisted.[14] So dangerous is this transition to the new world of deficiencies that the newborn is wrapped in a blanket to simulate the womb, kept warm in an even temperature, and allowed to sleep between feedings. Only when this basic need for security has been met is he free to strike out into a larger, more hazardous world and explore its boundless possibilities.

At first he will rage in terror at loss of support or withdrawal of the mother so essential to his sense of well-being. But the time is rapidly approaching when he will kick against the restraining blanket, struggle to turn over, and try to escape from the confining crib to explore the unknown world beyond his reach. Some inner need is urging him to gain freedom. Yet these strivings to be free and explore new possibilities are fraught with anxiety and ambiguity. He may strain at the leash in anxious longing to be free while at the same time he hesitates to leave the nest, and feels guilty to cast off from those on whom he depends for sustaining love.

[13] *Ibid.*, p. 181.
[14] Otto Rank, *The Trauma of Birth* (New York: Harcourt Brace, 1929).

No one has analyzed this anguishing dilemma between security and freedom more searchingly than Kierkegaard.[15] Human life begins in a state of dreaming innocence blissfully unconscious of danger and ignorant of its infinite possibilities. A growing person is a synthesis of the soul and the body, united in a third factor of potential awareness known as the spirit. Spirit is present at first in a state of immediacy or dreaming. Spirit is felt as a friendly power in its function of relating soul and body; yet it soon becomes a disturbing power which is experienced as dread. The body clamors to satisfy its hunger and lust, but it cannot be merely body or sink down into a vegetative existence, for the person is determined by spirit.

The person is at first innocent because he does not know. But he is not content to remain ignorant, for there is in him a spirit wanting to know. Like Adam and Eve he does not know at first the difference between good and evil. But he is tempted to know and taste the fruit of the tree of knowledge for himself. At the same time he dreads the spirit and the dangers into which his searching will lead him. He is ambivalent whether to reach out and forge ahead into the unknown or to retreat into the innocence and security of the past. The dread is a tension of the spirit seeking after adventure to penetrate the mystery, yet anxious and fearful of what may be found and its possible consequences.

Thus "dread is the dizziness of freedom" [16] which occurs when the free spirit gazes down into its own possibilities. In this moment it is as if I stood on the very edge of a precipice looking down into the abyss below. I sense that I am free to leap, and yet I dread leaping into the abyss of my own destruction. I now come to see that possibilities of a free spirit are infinite in contrast and consequences. How can I decide what to do if I have an impulse to leap into the unknown, yet know the danger of destroying myself and hurting others? As

[15] Søren Kierkegaard, *The Concept of Dread*, tr. Walter Lowrie (Princeton: Princeton University Press, 1944).
[16] *Ibid*, p. 55.

this dread rises before me, I may well decide to draw back into safety farther from the critical edge of this free choice.

Does this dread of freedom infect the scientist who rejects the possibility of freedom in favor of determinism? If everything in our universe operates according to natural law, how can a man claim that he is free? And by careful reasoning he builds an airtight case against freedom. The scientist once thought he was free in some earlier stage of innocence. He may even yet act as if he is free in forming his hypotheses and designing experiments and apparatus to explore the unknown. But then he may unite with other scientists in a theoretical defense of determinism, as a discipline imposed upon him by external facts. At the same time he may not see how his subjective needs and motives may affect his objectivity. Determinism of natural law gives a sense of security, for everything is predictable and can be known and verified by abstract reasoning (after we *assume* there is no freedom and enjoy the security of a deterministic paradise). Why blame me or anyone? How can we be held responsible in a world where every motion is predetermined?

Kierkegaard believed in freedom so much that he saw in every free person the dizziness and dread of our infinite possibilities, tempting us to sin in which the spirit could be overcome and yield its freedom to animal passion. One of the puzzling mysteries of his own life is why Kierkegaard renounced his engagement to marry the beautiful and desirable Regina. His analysis of freedom may offer clues to that mystery. He writes on "the fact that woman is more sensuous than man." [17] We may question this "fact," but let us see how Kierkegaard proceeds from there. To him the sensuous nature of woman is shown at once by her bodily organism. She is more beautiful than man; even when she is sleeping, her beauty is sensuously appealing.

Here we sense a note of dread when he continues: "Where beauty claims the right to rule it brings about a synthesis from which spirit is excluded." [18] This he illustrates from the whole

[17] *Ibid.*, p. 57.
[18] *Ibid.*, p. 58.

Hellenic culture in which he detects "a sense of security, a quiet solemnity which characterizes all Greek beauty because the spirit is excluded." This he sees as a sense of dread, a profound sorrow unexplained. Greek sensuousness is not viewed as sinfulness but an unexplained riddle which causes dread. Dread, he finds, is to be understood as oriented toward freedom. And such freedom may disregard the claims of spirit to fulfill the lusts of the body. The sexual itself is not sinful, but the forsaking of the spirit to indulge the body. "The dread of sin produces sin." [19] One succumbs to the impotence of dread precisely because he is both guilty and innocent.

The goal of woman is procreation, and even though she approaches it in dread, yet she is irresistibly drawn to fulfill her destiny. She will inevitably seduce the man, even though he is bashful and inhibited by shame. Eve tempts Adam by being there, and being what she is, a beautiful creature whose senuous nature is mingled with dread and desire. The dread of bashfulness revealed that the spirit felt itself foreign. When the spirit conquers, it views the sexual as foreign. In this conflict Kierkegaard seems to recoil from the sexual to the spiritual.

In Christianity the religious has suspended the erotic, not merely by an ethical understanding of it as sinful, but as the indifferent, because in spirit there is no difference between man and woman. Here the erotic is not ironically neutralized but suspended, because it is the tendency of Christianity to lead the spirit further. When in bashfulness the spirit is in dread and fear of arraying itself in the generic difference, the individual suddenly leaps away.[20]

This leaping away from the erotic he recognizes as the monastic view, implying that one in this predicament cannot stand the tension of opposites. To regain security he leaps to one extreme or the other. But why this dread? His reply is this: "Because in the culmination of the erotic the spirit cannot take part. I will speak here with Greek candor. The spirit indeed is present, for it is this which constitutes the synthesis

[19] *Ibid.*, p. 65.
[20] *Ibid.*, p. 63.

[of the whole person]. But it cannot express itself in the erotic experience; it feels itself a stranger." [21]

If we ask why not, he answers from his own unique subjectivity, his need to hold the spirit apart from the body, and his conviction that he must turn his back on the human love to commune in higher love with God alone as the Single One. Not *both/and* but *either/or* as he feels himself called away from all else but the divine. His spirit says, as it were, to the erotic: "My dear, I cannot be a third party here, therefore I will hide myself for the time being."

But this is precisely dread, and also this is precisely bashfulness; for it is a great stupidity to suppose that the wedding ceremony of the church, or the husband's fidelity in keeping himself unto her alone, is enough. Many a marriage has been profaned, and that not by an outsider. But when the erotic is pure and innocent and beautiful, the dread is friendly and mild, and therefore the poets are right in speaking about the sweet uneasiness.[22]

Evidently, his dread was not sweet and mild, but rather a pursuing fury or impotent fear that held him back from marriage. The freedom which he knew was essential to a happy marriage was somehow shadowed by dread and not within his grasp. Without that freedom he leaped to the security of the lonely spirit.

Søren was profoundly influenced by his father, a prosperous merchant who retired in his fortieth year to spend his life in study, meditation, and prayer. He was described by his son as the most melancholy man he had ever known and a very severe man. When Søren finally learned the secret which his father guarded in the deepest solitude, the son came to feel that he too lived under a family curse.

To such a degree is the whole foreground of my life enveloped in the darkest melancholy and in the clouds of a deeply brooding misery—no wonder I am what I am. . . . A fundamental melan-

---

[21] *Ibid.*, p. 64.
[22] *Ibid.*

choly, a tremendous dowry of suffering and this in the deepest sense sad, as a child educated by a melancholy old man.[23]

Søren had known Regina Olsen since he first met her in the home of friends when she was fourteen. He waited and they were engaged three years later in 1840, when he was twenty-seven years of age. He deeply loved her and hoped that marriage to her would lead him out of his melancholy. But he soon came to feel the engagement was a mistake, whether due to his melancholy, his reluctance to reveal himself and his past life, or a sense of sharp differences in personality and temperament. A year later he was evidently unable to reveal his inner secret to her.[24] He felt it would be fairer to take the blame upon himself by saying he no longer wanted to marry her. To make a clean break he left for Berlin, writing in his journal in 1841: "When the bonds were broken my thoughts were these: Either you throw yourself into the wildest kind of life—or else become absolutely religious, but it will be different from the parson's mixture." [25]

Perry LeFevre believes that when Kierkegaard broke the engagement to Regina, he was moved as in other decisive moments by a compelling sense of vocation to be a true Christian, in following Jesus by sacrificing whatever pleasures and personal commitments would bind him to compromise with the false and comfortable Christianity he must attack. Commenting on this break with Regina he wrote: "From that moment I dedicated my life with every ounce of my poor ability to the service of an idea." [26] After a long ambivalence he committed

[23] Kierkegaard, *Journals*, ed. and tr. Alexander Dru (London: Oxford University Press, 1938), p. 775.

[24] In 1843 he wrote: "If I should have explained myself to her I should have initiated her into terrible things, the relationship to my father, his melancholy, the eternal night that broods within, my despair, my passions, my going astray, which in God's eyes probably are not so terrible, for after all it was dread that made me go astray." *Ibid.*, p. 444.

[25] *Ibid.*, p. 337.

[26] *Ibid.*, p. 600. Quoted by Perry D. LeFevre, *The Prayers of Kierkegaard: Edited with a New Interpretation of His Life and Thought* (Chicago: University of Chicago Press, 1956), pp. 142-44.

himself to a self-denying life of speaking forth the truth at whatever cost. In this Christian vocation he was moving away from security to win a disciplined freedom which he believed to be his calling.

4. Intimacy or Isolation

Another anguishing dilemma confronting the growing person moves between intimacy or isolation. After a long and arduous struggle Kierkegaard, like his father, chose the path of isolation. Or in the perspective of his theology he chose isolation in human society to devote himself to intimacy with God. Others may undertake to mix the two or follow Hocking's law of alternation between the lonely vigil and social engagement. The urgent predicament of Kierkegaard was his need to take an absolute stand for his Christian vocation in terms of isolation.

Erikson finds this a characteristic dilemma of the young adult, and he relates it to the identity crisis. It is only when personal identity is well formed that true intimacy is possible. This refers to the capacity for sexual intimacy as well as intimacy in many other dimensions of one's social relationships. The youth who is not sure of his own identity will shy away from interpersonal intimacy in the form of friendship, combat, leadership, love, and mutual inspiration. Or he may throw himself into acts of intimacy which are promiscuous without deeply involving himself.

Where a youth does not accomplish such intimate relationships with others—and, I would add, with his own inner resources—in late adolescence or early adulthood, he may settle for highly stereotyped interpersonal relations and come to retain a deep *sense of isolation*. If the times favor an impersonal kind of interpersonal pattern, a man can go far, very far, in life and yet harbor a severe character problem doubly painful because he will never feel really himself, although everyone else says he is "somebody." [27]

[27] *Identity: Youth and Crisis*, pp. 135-36.

He may thus isolate himself in highly stereotyped and formal interpersonal relations, lacking in spontaneity, warmth, and real exchange of fellowship; or he will seek them frantically in repeated attempts and failures. Many young people who feel isolated flee into marriage, but find themselves isolated within their own home. Here they feel obliged to act in a defined way, as mates and parents, yet going through the motions of family life. They may give a hollow performance without truly finding themselves in finding one another. When Freud was asked what he thought a normal person should be able to do well, he replied: "To love and to work" (*Lieben und Arbeiten*). By love he meant generous intimacy, and by work he meant effective productivity, each in a freely spontaneous vital balance.

This crisis of the young adult is to feel drawn in opposite directions toward intimacy and isolation. There is a profound need to be loved and comforted and sustained by intimate relationships. Yet at the same time there is an anxious dread that draws us back from intimacy into the isolation of privacy and independence—to keep that distance at any cost. This ambivalence is acute in the relation of the young adult to his parents, upon whom he has depended since birth. He needs their love and longs for their approval and emotional support. And yet many families have lost the sense of intimacy and each person lives at home in isolated coexistence. This inner separation and need to be independent may drive a young man to leave home for good. A daughter may rush into marriage to leave home and escape her parents; and yet after marriage she may feel isolated from her husband and cling to her parents. These painful ambivalences must be worked through if the young person is to know who he is (identity) and maintain a wholesome balance (integrity) between these conflicting tensions.

Amae was a talented music major in a midwestern college, practicing long hours on the flute and piano. She was respected by her teachers as a good and faithful student who was heading for a promising career in music. This pleased her parents, who were musical and had had a family orchestra ever since the children were old enough to hold their instruments. She fell in love with Hai, who sat next to her in the flute section of the college orchestra. He was deeply involved in a premedical course, preparing to go to India as a medical missionary. His parents had long been interested in India, and put him in touch with the president of a Christian university, who came to see him and outlined the steps and timetable to follow in completing his preparation to teach and practice medicine in that university.

When he moved on to medical school in another state, he wrote letters faithfully and often came to see Amae. Eventually he asked her to marry him and they faced a dilemma.

"I do love you," she said seriously, "but what about my career in music?"

"Of course I wouldn't want you to give that up," Hai said. "Could you continue your music while I am completing the medical course, and then you would be prepared to teach music in the university where I will be in India?"

With this possibility in mind they did not check the course of their love, which had come to mean so much to them. They announced their engagement, and when she was soon to be graduated from college they set a wedding date, and plans were well along for the wedding. But three weeks before the wedding day a crisis arose.

Amae's father was taken ill with an unexpected heart attack which cast a foreboding shadow over the entire family. In the midst of his distress he called his daughter to his bedside and tearfully pleaded with her not to go to India.

"You know, Amae, how much you mean to me and your mother. We have set high hopes in your musical career, which will surely be blighted if you go to India."

"But, Father, I have promised Hai to go to India with him. The wedding day is only three weeks away, and we have already sent out the wedding invitations."

"Yes, I know, Amae. But how can I bear to have you so far away on the other side of the world! And now with my heart trouble, I will need you more than ever. And if I die your mother's heart will be broken not to have you near."

"Well, I see how you feel. But you know how much I love Hai."

"Yes, but why can't you ask him to change his plans? There are other places to practice medicine, and he could have an even greater career near home."

In the stress of sympathy for her father, now afflicted by this unexpected heart disease, and the sense of how much she owed the parents who had given her birth, nourished her growing life, and brought her to the threshold of a promising musical career, she did not know how to say no to her father's emotional appeal. Yielding to melting tears and mutual dependence in the family crisis which heightened her sense of obligation and primary loyalty to her family, who expected her to uphold their honor in a musical career, she promised to give up going to India.

Then hastening to her room, she wrote to Hai explaining the situation and confessing how she had promised her father to give up going to India. She begged his forgiveness and asked him to decide if they should go forward with the wedding on the day announced. She would be heartbroken if he said no, and yet she knew how much his medical career in India meant to him, and would accept whatever he decided was the right course to follow.

Hai was stunned by the surprising turn of events. How could he give up either his career or the girl he was going to marry? Hai leaned first one way and then the other, while Amae waited in anxious, guilty silence. He could see Amae and hear her pleading words, knowing how much she counted upon him and wanted to fulfill their life together. He felt he must be true to her, and when they were married they could work out the future step by step.

They were married on the appointed day with both families present for the wedding. There was rejoicing in the joining of man and wife "until death do us part." Yet there was an undertone of tragic sadness, knowing the rift that had come between them. But they were trying to forget the hidden conflict and rise above it to hope that love would conquer all difficulties. Still there were hidden doubts: Have we moved ahead too fast, have we taken the right step, or should we have waited until the conflict of careers and families might be worked through to deeper understanding and unity, that we might stand in the light instead of this uneasy shadow?

To all appearances they were perfectly adjusted and completely devoted to each other. And they kept up the rituals of devotion to reassure each other and overwhelm their own doubts. Yet in his private thoughts Hai knew how deep was his sorrow in giving up the career to which he had been committed in India. And in her heart Amae could not really feel light and free, for the shadow of guilt was heavy, that she had deeply wounded him in forcing him to set aside his career for her. Have I asked too much of him? And can our love ever be the same or truly fulfill our highest hopes?

Consequently, the intimacy each had hoped for in the other was somehow, in spite of all their efforts, denied them. Whether at work or love they could not give all of themselves in that profound sense of wholeness that always eluded them. They were tasting the bitterness of inner isolation from each other, and from the work that each felt called to do. If love and work are both hollow, where then can one find fulfillment?

The stress and strain of such unfulfilling efforts began to take their toll. Each one worked harder to accomplish less, and they exerted themselves to love more while enjoying it less. Fatigue and futility were creeping into the daily rhythm of life. Amae became so exhausted she gave up her musical studies and remained in bed. Hai was on night duty in the emergency ward, but he hurried home day after day to prepare and serve her meals. He could see how much this extra attention meant to her, with her longing to be loved. It seemed almost, but not quite, like the intimacy she hoped for in marriage.

When he accepted an invitation to practice medicine in Nebraska, they settled into their new home in time for the delivery of a son. Here they began a new life together as a family of three, drawn by the hope that the intense suffering and longing for each other would now come to fulfillment. Becoming a mother opened a new dimension of intimacy for Amae, who was very close to little Kris in nursing and rocking him to sleep. She lay aside her arduous practice of the flute which had once occupied so many hours of the day and gave herself fully to the rhythm of her baby's needs, almost as if they lived one life from heartbeat to heartbeat.

This was going to be the best time of their life, as they settled into their home, thankful to be together to give and receive their love, and now drawn into the intimate sharing of life with their son and each other. They were freer to relax and accept the intimacy of family life. It was a year of fulfillment, when the anguish of former conflict vanished, and they shared the love they both desired.

I have chosen symbolic names for them from the Japanese. *Amae* means the need to be loved and the hungering for a dependent relationship to one who loves you intimately. Each of them had learned from birth to depend on their parents as now little Kris was depending on them for love. Yet as they came to young adulthood, they strove for independence to assert their will and decide for themselves who they would be. Amae's father at a moment of illness was unable to give her up and claimed her continuing love and nearness at a time when she needed to be free to make her independent decisions.

Hai in that crisis turned one way and the other, and seemed unable to decide for himself. His name in Japanese means "Yes." Not yet asserting the full strength of his manhood, he said yes to both alternatives in a contradictory sense. Out of this confusion he said yes to Amae to marry at whatever cost to his career in India. He intended this yes to be a wholehearted affirmation of her as his wife and of himself as her husband. But unconsciously he had conflicting feelings which defeated both his affirmation of her and of himself as a physician within the limits of these confining boundaries. His yes was verbal and audible, but his whole being was not in it.

161

He was tortured in the identity of his yes, as she was tortured in the identity of a person needing both to love and be loved.

5. Doubt or Faith

Then came a shock to shatter the wholeness of this new life in Nebraska. Hai contracted pneumonia, and the Xrays showed a spreading tuberculosis in his lungs. He was placed immediately in a local sanatorium, and his medical associate prescribed complete rest with every appropriate treatment available to his condition. During that year he was cheerful and optimistic about his recovery. The medical director, however, was not so optimistic; and Amae was always near by, with her son Kris, to see him as often as possible and be available in any way she might be needed. Three months later he had a severe coughing spell and died in her arms. When the families gathered for the memorial service, they talked over the future, and she decided to return to her musical studies.

Within a year she came to an acute health crisis, which was diagnosed as tuberculosis, and she had many months of complete rest in a sanatorium. She was heard to say: "I would like to be with Hai in heaven; I feel closer to him than anyone on earth."

When she recovered she moved with her son to a city to become a music teacher. She went from door to door to recruit pupils and taught them well. But the income was insufficient and her resources dwindled until she was in dire straits. She struggled day after day to do her work and be a good mother to Kris. Yet she met emptiness wherever she turned.

At this moment in her life she was assailed by all the anguishing dilemmas we have confronted in this chapter. Anxiety arose in these crises to shake the foundations of trust on which she stood in the whirling tide of tragic events. She was attacked by a deep sense of guilt that she may have been the cause in one way or another of Hai's death. In her desire for security in her family, had she not constricted his freedom and driven him into a distress that made him vulnerable to fatal illness? Had she burdened their marriage by her own illness, feelings of insecurity, and dependence on him for emotional support?

Recalling the emptiness of her isolation since his illness and death, and times of inner separation in their early marriage, had she failed to meet his need for intimacy? Even her effort to meet her father's need for intimate security in his illness had boomeranged. For she felt estranged from him in feeling he had asked too much of her. Capturing for a moment the joy of that first intimacy with baby Kris, she was now painfully aware of his growing independence and unwillingness to be "good little boy," as when he once snuggled in her arms.

This terrible sense of isolation did not become easier as the days passed into years. There was no "healing power of time," as one comforter had said too glibly. For as she struggled on without achieving her major goals, she felt helplessly alone and hopelessly defeated. Why had every devotion failed and every struggle come to naught? What of the faith that in spite of everything had carried her so far? Where was that firm ground on which she had stood when she believed that God was there to help and care for them and answer the fervent prayer? Her faith was trembling and shaken by growing doubts. Yet though earth might fail, she had not doubted Hai was there in heaven waiting to welcome her.

On that day when Kris returned from school he called as usual, but there was no answer. Where could Mother be? Looking around he saw a piece of note paper on the Bible. Opening it he read the message she had left for him. "I have tried my best but there is no other way. You will be better cared for by your grandparents who have invited you to come and live with them. Good-bye, I am going to heaven to live with your father."

The son Kris remembers his mother as a woman of great faith in spite of the anguish and doubts that assailed her. He recalls on the morning of her death she read to him from the Bible:

163

> Bless the Lord, O my soul,
>   and forget not all his benefits,
> who forgives all your iniquity,
>   who heals all your diseases. . . .
> For as the heavens are high above the earth,
>   so great is his steadfast love toward
>   those who fear him;
> as far as the east is from the west,
>   so far does he remove our transgressions
>   from us. (Psalm 103.)

Kris thinks of himself as "the child of two deaths," and devotes his life to carrying forward their search for faith and love, which was intensified by the tragic conflict they wrestled to resolve. His mother was so deeply moved by Hai's illness and death that she identified with him in suffering tuberculosis and death. She brushed aside every thought of marrying again and chose the way of Madame Butterfly to be faithful even to death.

We are reminded by Erikson that every stage of growth has its own crisis, and the final crisis of growth in the later years is integrity versus despair.[28] In this stage there are cumulative losses to bear, and a final coming to terms with oneself before the finality of death. Will we surrender to despair and let life slip like sand through our fingers? Or shall we gather up the resources of our whole life into a culminating, unyielding integrity that affirms life and takes responsibility for what has been and what has to come?

Tillich also reminds us that a dynamic faith can never be free of doubt, which is the essential counterpoint that intensifies the struggle to achieve an undefeatable faith.[29] Here as in every other of life's anguishing dilemmas, a vital balance is needed to integrate these conflicting counterforces into a complex unity of a living and growing wholeness.

[28] *Identity and the Life Cycle*, p. 98.
[29] *The Dynamics of Faith* (New York: Harper, 1957), p. 18. "Doubt is a necessary element in [faith]. It is a consequence of the risk of faith." "The doubt which is implicit in faith accepts this insecurity and takes it into itself as an act of courage" (p. 20).

Erikson speaks of his own loneliness and sense of uprootedness in migrating from his homeland to a new country. There
is a natural period of uprootedness in human life at the turning
point from youth to adulthood. "Like a trapeze artist, the
young person in the middle of vigorous motion must let go
of his safe hold on childhood and reach out for a firm grasp
on adulthood." [30] For a breathless interval he must depend on
a relatedness between past and future. He must at that moment
depend on the reliability of those he must let go and of those
who will receive him. Then young people must become whole
in their own right by achieving a new sense of inner identity.

This transmigration was the intense inner struggle of Hai
and Amae, who were uprooted as much as if they had left their
homeland for India on the other side of the world. After that
critical moment of indecision when she promised her father
not to go, each one was cut off from the past in the crisis of
their emancipation. They moved uneasily to achieve a new
identity in becoming a family of three in another city to bring
healing to other sufferers. Then illness intervened as a tragic
disaster, to separate them in death and shatter their new family
identity.

From that time on Amae and little Kris were uprooted and
homeless persons. By a series of renewed efforts Amae gave
her energies to achieving identity as a musician and teacher.
Each time she met defeat and moved to another city in search
of a homeland. Yet to her there was no homeland for her
spirit except in the identity she and Hai had formed together.
In their faithfulness to each other she was fulfilled in fidelity
to him in life and death.

Kris was also uprooted as "the child of two deaths," and
migrated from place to place in search of his home. He belongs
to a whole generation of young and older persons who are in
transmigration from a past that is no longer theirs into a new
world where they feel like homeless strangers. Whether we
dwell in crowded cities or set foot on the moon, we know the

---

[30] *Insight and Responsibility*, p. 90.

anguishing dilemmas of growth. We know the loneliness of outgrowing a life where once we were at home, in search of a new world that may find us homeless. Like Augustine we may confess, "Our hearts are restless until they find rest in Thee."

Anguishing dilemmas of growth can spell either victory or defeat for the person. Whether he becomes a winner or a loser largely depends upon his prevailing self-concept. The person's self-concept is deeply affected by his view of the world. If he is basically trusting and hopeful, the person is able to face reversals in strength and turn apparent defeat into victory.

Otherwise, anxiety may turn into despair, guilt into self-condemnation and debilitating self-effacement. Preoccupation with obsessive, compulsive security-seeking operations cheat the person from realizing his freedom. All such loser reactions tend to shut off the flow of personal consciousness, greatly restricting the person's life space.

Faith enables a person to live his life as a winner, because any experience is transformed into an opportunity for him. He perceives possibilities for learning and growth in what seems to be a reversal. He learns to appreciate and to appropriate his own strengths. Thus, although he continues to experience anxiety, guilt, and threats to his freedom on occasion, he does not acquiesce to his negative feelings. On the contrary, he experiences them fully—he really allows himself *to feel* them— hence, he is not shattered by them. He becomes strengthened by each such experience for enduring the next, and so on.

Faith is not a magic solution to life's problems, or a placebo for pains, or a spiritual tranquilizer which forms an implacable cocoon around the believers. It is a depth of commitment to a genuinely trusting relationship, rooted in the central assurance of the validity of love in the world.

We will turn next to exploring adventures of faith through which the verities of love are realized in a person's life. We will examine the ways in which each adventure becomes an occasion for renewal and transformation. Then we will see how such changed persons become agents of change in the communities of which they are a part.

VIII

Adventures in Christian Faith

When a person makes a decision in relation to dilemmas he faces, he inevitably opens up a series of adventures. These adventures involve risk and excitement. Acting in love toward other persons is an adventure that is both frightening and fulfilling for the person initiating the action.

If the person is not strictly automated—always acting in ways for which he is programmed by early experiences and by the technical culture—he actualizes his freedom by entering into such adventures. Thus he becomes open to his own growth potential.

Encounters are calls to adventure. Our responses shape the character of our existence. A series of such adventures make up the pilgrimage of our lives. John Bunyan's *Pilgrim's Progress* is a classic example of an effort to portray adventures in Christian faith. Some modern writings also convey the notion of life as a pilgrimage.

In his book *The Hero with a Thousand Faces*, Joseph Campbell says the effect of the hero's (Everyman's) adventure is to unlock and release again "the flow of life into the body of the world." The creative effect of the hero's adventure, therefore, is a revitalizing of the people to whom he returns.

A hero ventures forth from the world of common day into a region of supernatural wonder: fabulous forces are there encountered and a decisive victory is won: the hero comes back from this mysterious adventure with the power to bestow boons on his fellow man.[1]

Psychoanalysts would see the adventure as an encounter between the ego and the unconscious forces which threaten to overwhelm the ego. The victory in such encounters expands awareness and personal consciousness, thus releasing the creativity of the person. His gifts to his fellowmen are increased capacity for organizing, systemizing, and developing new structures for the dynamic systems operating within and around them.

How do we talk about these adventures? We use concepts to symbolize what we are experiencing. Adventures of faith, for example, involve us with others in a community of experiencing, interpreting, and celebrating events. We reflect upon these events. They teach us and enrich us as we are able to conceptualize them.

We speak of love as the source of all life. We not only derive this notion from our relationships, we intuitively appropriate God's creative love. We also experience that love breaking upon us, enabling us to give up the conditions we put on our worth. Thus we are loved into being. We realize more of ourselves than we dreamed possible. Our own potential for self-giving is actualized, and our creativity is activated.

However, what do we mean by the word "love"? Is it a wonderfully ambiguous term which says everything yet nothing? Is love the problem rather than the answer to our problems?

Love is not just a pleasant feeling, but the vital energy in relationships. It is a precondition for forgiveness, which makes relationships between caring people possible. What is the nature of forgiveness? In what ways do we misunderstand what is meant by forgiveness? How does forgiveness promote reconciliation?

When we become reconciled to others and to God, do we

[1] (New York: Meridian Books, 1956), p. 40.

assume that everything will now be rosy? Do we naïvely feel that as long as we affirm each other's right to be, things will turn out for the best? The young couple, for example, who are sure they are meant for each other get married and begin to live together. They have committed themselves to an enduring relationship. What does such a commitment mean? Suppose they soon begin to doubt their original feelings of compatibility. What, now, does their commitment to each other imply? What do we mean by ultimate commitment?

What is really worthy of our commitment? Our institutions? Are they not so deficient as to fail miserably to serve us? The person is deeply affected by the communities to which he relates. No real understanding of him is possible apart from a study of the system of interactions among such communities. Nor can we understand him without carefully viewing the history of the communities to which he is loyal. How may they be reformed?

The questions we raise regarding the concepts we form and the institutions we create to implement them lead us into adventures of faith in search of intelligent and consistent answers. Thus we hope so to order our existence that we may realize a genuine fulfillment, which is the true reward for our search. Yet, in the ordering we intend to remain vitally open to the continuing creative activity of God.

1. Love and Creativity

Creativity is the act of assimilating, testing, organizing, and implementing what has exploded into consciousness. A novel idea or reorganized set of ideas, an invention, an aesthetic expression, a depth of feeling, an illumined spirit are phrases that are used to define creativity and to describe its function. Love provides the impetus to creativity. Creativity is the fruition of love. Creativity is a term which encompasses the whole process of becoming conscious of possibilities and taking steps to actualize them.

Toynbee has said: "Potential creative behavior can be stifled, stunted, and stultified by the prevalence in society of adverse attitudes of mind and habits of behavior." [2] We are suggesting that such adverse attitudes are generated by resentment and hate. Adverse habits of behavior are the output of resentment. Or to put the matter positively and to present the thesis here: Love engenders attitudes of mind and habits of behavior which release potential creativity.

Empirical studies lend verification to our thesis that love generates creativity. J. H. McPherson, in a study of the effect of environment on creativity, found that "a scientist's creativity is the result of a fortunate combination of intellectual characteristics, emotional dispositions, and a particular climate that is favorable for him." [3] A relevant point of this study in showing the interrelationship between love and creativity was the conclusion: "A scientist who is able to use the major mental factors effectively and who is problem-centered, spontaneous, and independent may thrive in a supportive and stimulating environment but flounder in a hostile climate." [4] This documents empirically what Toynbee had postulated in a philosophical vein: Potential creativity can be shut off in a hostile and destructive environment. We are saying it can be activated and facilitated by love, which creates the conditions for creativity.

We are now faced, then, with the task of saying what we mean by love. Love as a meaningful term has almost become a modern contradiction. In fact, in his acutely perceptive analysis of love and will, Rollo May asserts they themselves have become the problems rather than the answer ot the predicaments of our day.[5] They have become the problems largely

---

[2] Arnold Toynbee, "Creative Minority," in *Widening Horizons in Creativity*, ed. Calvin W. Taylor (New York: John Wiley, 1964), p. 3.

[3] "Environment and Training for Creativity," in *Creativity: Progress and Potential*, ed. C. W. Taylor (New York: McGraw-Hill, 1964), p. 130.

[4] *Ibid.*

[5] *Love and Will* (New York: W. W. Norton, 1969), p. 13.

because they have been offered in the past as the answers to life's struggles and uncertainties. For example, love has been such an elusive, will-o-the-wisp to people who have judged their worthiness on whether or not they had achieved it, that it has become disillusioning. To some, it has even been regarded as a facade for a subtle controlling and manipulating force employed by the clever or the more powerful. In that sense, the term has fallen into disrepute. For others, love has seemed a disheartening illusion, as unattainable as the enchanting pot of gold at the end of a rainbow. At any rate, May concludes that love has become a problem to itself.

Nevertheless, genuine love is the source of all creativity. Creation itself—bringing order out of chaos—is an act of love. Calling another into being is an expression of love.

Genuine love calls us into being. Stimulating an organism into being is a creative act. The love of a man and woman for each other, for example, draws out the manhood and womanhood of each. The love of a mother for her child brings him out as a being capable of self-giving love and caring service on his own. By loving and encouraging their children to realize their creative potential, both parents are to that degree fulfilling their own. The latter statement is not meant to suggest a symbiotic attachment of parents to children—parents trying to push children to certain goals which they have set for themselves, thus hoping to get fulfillment through their children. The fulfillment of the vocation of parenthood is in the support and encouragement of their children's *own* creative interests and possibilities. Such is an act of love.

Love as Subjectivity

Passion for truth and meaning impels the lover to single-minded devotion to the object. His valuings may not make sense to the outsider. Only as the other is able to experience for himself what is valued can he give himself to it. Kierkegaard, for example, emphasized the subjective love of truth as a corrective to the dehumanizing nature of scientific objectification. His concern for passion and faith, which is being

171

stressed today and continually expressed by groups who are concerned to make a witness, is indeed pertinent to our times. However, he seemed to conclude that objectivity was not at all applicable to religion and not at all compatible with passion and faith. His reaction to rationalism was so extreme that he was blinded to the creative potential in the subjective-objective tension. Nevertheless, he put important stress on the need for an inward attitude which is wholeheartedly honest and basically trustful. Lest I give the impression that I am interpreting Kierkegaard's views on love as sentimental—inclined toward the feelings or emotions—I hasten to add: His meaning is just the opposite. The very title of one set of discourses, *Works of Love*, suggests love in the sense of duty and action. To love one's neighbor is to do something to meet his needs, not just to have good feelings about him.

In modern expressions of existentialism—in Jean-Paul Sartre for example—love, like human existence per se, is destined to continual frustration. Love drives the person to try to engulf the freedom of the other person. Once he succeeds he defeats himself, because then the other person ceases to be a person. Love, which is an attempt to overcome isolation and alienation, is the freedom which separates human beings from one another. The lover tries to become the source of ultimate meaning to the beloved, to be the all in all, the absolute to the other. His victory is his defeat and the cause for frustration. Seemingly, therefore, the liberty engendered by love is a kind of curse. However, Sartre does not see it that way. Freedom, which is the cause of a man's estrangement and alienation from other men and from other things, is also the source of his creativity. The dynamics would seem to be love–freedom–creativity. Sartre gives the impression that he resents the fact that he must relinquish the Godlike omnipotence of infancy for the sake of the maturity which grants the freedom of others. Yet Sartre's views raise the question of whether or not one's mutual fruition can be obtained through affirming the freedom of others. Is there evidence of love in creation? Does the merging of two, interacting free souls result in the creative event?

172

Love as Intentionality

Love is creative in the sense that love is the force or power which underlies what we intend to happen. Rollo May observes that love and will are interdependent in efficacy. He shows how love and will can block each other. Will can be manipulative. Love can be too generalized and dissociating. They function together to plumb the depths and meaning of interpersonal relationships; consequently, man's abiding task is to unite love and will as a part of conscious development. Quoting James Baldwin's prophetic hope for effective transformations in race relations through a new consciousness, May says, "Both love and will are ways of creating consciousness in others. To be sure, each may be abused: love may be used as a way of clinging, and will as a way of manipulating others in order to enforce a compliance." [6] Nevertheless, the expression of love is a way of producing a change in others, of expanding and deepening consciousness in others and in ourselves.

An event in a high school in a large metropolitan area was almost inevitably doomed to end in tragic consequences. Two sixteen-year-old boys had come to a showdown. An angry group of supporters of one of the boys was urging him to kill the other boy. With his knife drawn, he seemed intent on doing just that. In fact, he was keenly aware of the social pressure being exerted on him. If he backed down, he would lose so much face with his peers that he would wish he were dead. He had no alternative but to defend his honor and risk his life.

Many students, not directly involved, were a short distance from the tense encounter, watching in shocked silence. They dimly realized they were about to observe what seemed to be certain violence and almost as surely the death of one of their fellow students. They had heard of it happening frequently in street fights and even in some of the other schools. Now, they were witnessing firsthand. As one observer said later, "I was really scared. I could just see it happening. And there I was froze."

[6] *Ibid.*, p. 309.

Suddenly, one of the young women teachers who had come to the scene moved quietly but quickly to confront the boy who was holding the knife. Looking him in the eye steadily but warmly, without raising her voice, she called him by name and said simply, "We love you, and we love Raoul too. Now, please, give me the knife." He glared at her for a moment, his bulky frame towering over her. He was so shocked at the kindness and softness in her voice, which contrasted with the harshness and yelling he usually experienced from adults, that he could say nothing to her. After what she confessed later seemed like an eternity, his tense body relaxed and he handed her the knife. She rushed to him and embraced him, holding him tightly to her. Many young people who had been watching in stunned silence, expressing feelings of both relief and gratitude, began to weep.

The young teacher had ably communicated her intention, which was to bring about reconciliation through love. Perhaps a similar act would not be effective again in the same situation. Maybe it would not be needed in that particular group with that teacher present. At any rate, these are not the moot points in question. At this time love as intentionality *was effective*, because love was genuine and appropriate. Courage was in the act, but it was born less of confidence in the power of authority and more of the authority of genuine love.

The teacher could trust her own feelings because she was assured of their genuineness. She said later, "Boy, was I scared! I had no idea what I would do or say. I didn't even think about that. I just said to myself, I will go in there because I know my motive is love. I trust that. If that doesn't work, nothing will. Love is at stake here!" With that she found herself walking calmly to confront the hate and violence which had erupted.

The boy found that his peers were as touched by the courage and faith of the young teacher as he was. He had not lost face by changing his resolve! As the young people engaged in animated discussion of their experience later in the class with the teacher, he found the strength to say that he was glad she stopped him. Softly, he almost whispered from his bowed head, while his fellow students wept around him, he had never known such love. This was not "soft-headed" sentimentality. It was a genuine self-giving from which everyone learned the strength of love.

Helmut Thielicke speaks of the creative power of love as *agape*: "Agape is not a response to a 'loveworthiness' which is already there; it is rather the creative cause that produces this 'loveworthiness' " [7] Using the analogy of the photographer's art in employing catalysts to bring the picture into view, Thielicke describes a similar effect of the lover upon his beloved. Whether or not the analogy does justice to the complex process of calling the other into being, it illustrates the creativity in love as intentionality. The development of the capacity to perceive possibilities and to reach out to remake, to form, and to reform, not as manipulation,—to make what is there what I want it to be—but as creation—to bring out what is there to become what it potentially is seeking to be.

Love as Incarnation

The idea of "putting on one's neighbor" is incomprehensible to many modern people. The notion of taking on the joys, sorrows, happiness, disappointment, victories, defeats, sufferings, of other people seems strangely incongruous with contemporary experience, if not naïvely preposterous. We have already commented on Rollo May's observation that love has become a problem to itself. The world we live in suffers sorely from apathy and anesthesia in the sense of lack of feelings. Even constructive pain seems gone in some instances, or at least we do not know the source of the pain we experience.

Yet, we are deeply aware that the way to cure this "warring madness in our members" is to participate fully in the lives of others. The extending of our consciousness of the world requires this. Real participation inevitably means self-revelation. Consciousness of others and of the world is increased through mutual revelation. This is the meaning of love as incarnation.

[7] *The Ethics of Sex* (New York: Harper, 1964), p. 32.

The young teacher who courageously risked herself for the sake of reconciling her students was manifesting the incarnation of love. Her action expressed what she felt deeply as well as what, intellectually, she believed to be true. She was not simply mouthing the words of love; she was consistently manifesting love with her very being. She was not acting out of a fundamentally alienated need to control which, in effect, says, "I can't trust you. You are no good. Therefore, I have to suppress you, to keep your evil from getting out of hand." Rather, she was offering her love as a genuine gift of herself. Her offering of herself was consistent with her life style. The boy knew this and was moved by it. He saw no fraud or pretense. He was confronted by love incarnate and had to respond. He might kill it, but he would run the risk of killing the only hope for love in himself.

In the Incarnation, God meets man where he is and lures him to quicken his consciousness of the world. Man is continually called to revitalize his focus of expressing his awareness for this encounter. Creativity is the result of that struggle. "So the Word of God became flesh; he came to dwell among us, and we saw his glory, such glory as befits the Father's only Son, full of grace and truth." (John 1:14 NEB.) Only as we experience the incarnation of the significant other can we "see" his glory. His truth—the reality of his being—comes through to us and breaks into our consciousness.

Love and creativity are united in the Incarnation. Our creative possibilities are actualized in our every act of becoming incarnate—of taking on the "flesh" of essential humanity, or living in the life of another and letting him live in me. Self-revelation and the incorporating of the other revealed self are the requisite acts toward achieving greater consciousness. Creativity is the action of giving formal expression to the vitality generated from this, the true meaning of the dynamic of love.

2. Forgiveness and Reconciliation

To many people forgiveness means only what a minimal definition offers, to give up resentment against another, to pardon, or to relinquish the desire to punish. The implication is that someone offends and the other pardons him. The easy assumption is that the "righteous" ones forgive those who go astray. The fact that "all sin and fall short of the glory of God" is neither understood nor taken seriously. In fact, such language in itself seems archaic and meaningless to moderns who are woefully disturbed about riots and violence, but often do not really know the young people who are "causing" them. The solemn acts of pardon and the offers of release for punishment are still the acts of the righteous ones. If they can admit their long hair is disgraceful and their hippie clothes outlandish, we can take them back into fellowship. This seems to be the attitude of the standpat generation. Youth counter with the hope that older people will renounce their materialistic values, give up some of their stifling power, and relax their "uptight" views.

Forgiveness is an expression of love. This has clearly been the tone of biblical references to the term. I think Mowrer misses the essential point of the concept of forgiveness when he calls it an "ambiguous and bloody" doctrine, on the grounds that it promotes a cheap and easy grace. His assumption seems to be that the teaching of forgiveness promotes a kind of permissiveness which is detrimental to character. Such interpretations of forgiveness deserve his criticism because they are gross distortions of the true meaning of forgiveness.

Contrary to Mowrer's interpretation of forgiveness as an "act of condescension and not at all likely to restore either our self-respect or peace of mind," [8] I see the responsible interaction growing out of forgiveness as producing strong character and self-respect. Of course, we must say what we are talking about when we use the word "forgiveness." Forgiveness is the act of offering oneself to the other unconditionally in faith and trust. Neither faith nor trust is possible, nor can a relationship be genuine, unless real repentance has taken place. Repentance is literally a turning around. We cannot face each other until

[8] O. Hobart Mowrer, *The Crisis in Psychiatry and Religion* (New York: Van Nostrand, 1961), p. 196.

we turn toward each other. This is more than a symbolic gesture. Responsibility is required.

However, in the light of what we have already said about love, genuine forgiveness is participation. Forgiveness is manifest in increasing consciousness of others and the world. This is not done through propounding arguments in self-justification but in genuine participation. No one can say he truly *knows* another without participating in his life. Parents are much more prone to be critical of their children, true, but also to forgive them more readily than are others who really do not know them. Forgiveness makes love possible, love makes forgiveness genuine. Out of the interaction between forgiveness and love comes reconciliation.

In a poignant and moving encounter with a whore in a Pharisee's house (an incongruous situation, to say the least), Jesus was reported to have taught a humble lesson of forgiveness.

One of the Pharisees invited him to dinner to eat with him; he went to the Pharisee's house and took his place at table. A woman who was living an immoral life in the town had learned that Jesus was at table in the Pharisee's house and had brought oil of myrrh in a small flask. She took her place behind him, by his feet, weeping. His feet were wetted with her tears and she wiped them with her hair, kissing them and anointing them with the myrrh. When his host the Pharisee saw this he said to himself, "If this fellow were a real prophet, he would know who this woman is that touches him, and what sort of woman she is, a sinner." Jesus took him up and said, "Simon, I have something to say to you." "Speak on, Master," said he. "Two men were in debt to a money-lender: one owed him five hundred silver pieces, the other fifty. As neither had anything to pay with he let them both off. Now, which will love him most?" Simon replied, "I should think the one that was let off most." "You are right," said Jesus. Then turning to the woman, he said to Simon, "You see this woman? I came to your house: you provided no water for my feet; but this woman has made my feet wet with her tears and wiped them with her hair. You gave me no kiss; but she has been kissing my feet ever since I came in. You did not anoint my head with oil; but she has anointed my feet with myrrh. And so, I tell you, her great love proves that her many sins have been forgiven; where little has been forgiven, little love is shown." Then he said to her, "Your sins are forgiven." The other guests began to ask themselves, "Who is this, that he can forgive sins?" But he said to the woman, "Your faith has saved you; go in peace." (Luke 7:36-50 NEB.)

The rather endless pratings about who is right and who is wrong miss the point of the implications for forgiveness in this story. This statement is not meant to obscure the reality of a rightness and a wrongness. To understand another is not to give tacit approval for his behavior. Wrong is wrong and sin is sin. Furthermore, there are indeed the righteous. Righteousness is not just bestowed, but comes at a tremendous price. Rigorous discipline, persistence in labor, self-control, and much stocktaking is required. A man usually is highly estimated and given status as a leader in his group or in his community because he has demonstrated his dependability and responsibility. He has shown he is faithful to trust. However, if he uses his position of status to dominate and control others in whose welfare he has little interest, his "righteousness" is under judgment.

In the story Jesus did not minimize the woman's sins or explain them away. Sinners are sinners, and he saw them as such: "Her *many* sins are forgiven." The righteous are righteous. There was no equivocation about them either. Jesus used both terms without slurring over them. However, he took the side of the sinner against the righteous while affirming the demands of the law, which the righteous struggle to protect.

Here, Jesus was teaching the paradoxical truth of Christian faith. The sense of sin is positive and constructive, because it enables people to experience reconciliation through forgiveness. "Just so long as we deny the reality of sin," says Mowrer, "we cut ourselves off, it seems, from the possibility of radical redemption (recovery)." [9] I would interpret the latter phrase as implying that we cut ourselves off from the possibility of forgiveness and reconciliation which is radically redemptive. We deny ourselves the richness of an expanded consciousness.

[9] *Ibid.*, p. 40.

179

Though we are rich (in wealth and acquisition), we are poor (impoverished in consciousness).

Forgiveness is not based on conditions. It does not depend on what we have done or have not done. Jesus did not say that "you may be forgiven, if you do so and so"; he said: "Your many sins *are* forgiven." He was not questioning her motives, but perceiving the genuine character of her love. Obviously, the woman had *already* experienced forgiveness. She *knew* she was accepted. The reality came as refreshing rain on parched ground.

Her tears symbolized her overwhelming gratitude at the realization that another life is possible! One is not totally condemned. "There is therefore now no condemnation," the apostle Paul affirmed in concluding his statement on faith, "for those who are in Christ Jesus" (Rom. 8:1). Consciousness of this reality is experienced as a tremendous release of anxiety and a birth of hope.

To what extent can one endure the lack of response to forgiveness? What are the limits of reasonableness in a forgiving spirit?

"How many times do you expect me to take you back?" the young wife challenged her errant husband in a marital counseling session. Silent and displaying an attitude of indifference, he shrugged his shoulders. "Well, you keep calling me up after each one of your escapades and asking me if you can crawl back. And I melt and give in. How long do you think I can keep that up?" As I heard this, my mind was playing on the fact that she seemed to be questioning seriously the validity of forgiving "seventy times seven." Actually, however, he was not truly asking for forgiveness, but to take him back as an unrepentant sinner.

"If I let you come back again," the woman continued, "I am going to be sure that your intentions are right." She was seeking to generate in him a sense of responsibility to her faith and trust. She knew intuitively that the genuine response to forgiveness is commitment. Sincere repentance and deep commitment open a person to an appropriation of the grace of God, to which we turn next in our discussion of the adventures in Christian faith.

3. Commitment and Grace

Grace is the loving action of God toward man; commitment is the response of man to that grace. Creative transformation of a person occurs as grace is appropriated and commitment is affirmed. However, this does not happen automatically or in a vacuum. Grace is from other people, and commitment involves other people as well as oneself. Commitment, therefore, is a condition of total responsibility.

In his discussion of the relationship between love and will, Rollo May shows how love may block will. In the hippie movement, he notes, love is regarded as indiscriminate. May rightfully sees the attitude displayed as a reaction against the manipulative will of the previous generation. The pleas for "immediacy, spontaneity, and honesty" in relationships are convincing indictments of the manipulative love and sex in a bourgeois culture. However, love requires encounter of person with person, spirit with spirit, in depth over a period of time.[10]

Conflict and growth are essential to achieving a depth of love. They require choice and will. You choose one and not another. You encounter the other in conflict, and you grow by virtue of that encounter. Not to know anyone intimately in depth is not to know anyone! To know one in depth is inevitably to experience conflict and to realize one's growth potential.

Choice and will are the active expressions of freedom. Commitment is the exercising of choice and will in a responsible relationship. Commitment is directional; it requires the goal of a future direction—"to" or "unto"—to complete it. In any intention its directional sense is implied. Choice indicates the focusing of commitments. Will is the staying power essential to being committed to anything or anybody. To choose means

[10] *Love and Will*, p. 278.

to make a decision, which is the act of cutting off the possibilities of other choices. Indecisiveness is the inability to choose an alternative, thus, in a real sense, forestalling growth.

We begin with grace, because by the grace of God, our beginnings are possible. Like Paul, we may find grace as the gift of God's love and mercy entrusted to us as a treasure. "We are no better than pots of earthenware to contain this treasure," the apostle Paul wrote, in what seems to be a disparaging tone in a letter to the people of Corinth (II Cor. 4:7 NEB). But he had already affirmed the glory of such incarnation: "We all reflect as in a mirror the splendor of the Lord; thus we are transfigured into his likeness" (II Cor. 3:18a NEB). Furthermore, he is reminded of the responsibility to which the appropriation of grace calls us! "Seeing then we have been entrusted with this commission, which we owe entirely to God's mercy, we never lose heart." (II Cor. 4:1-2 NEB.)

Commitment, then, is the condition of being entrusted with a sacred commission. If we are faithful, we are rewarded with the great gift of expanding consciousness—the enrichment of an increased awareness. If we are miserly with the grace we receive and try to possess it or own it for ourselves, we forfeit it. This is basically the reality to which Jesus was pointing as he described the kingdom of heaven in his parable of the good and trusty servants (Matt. 25:14-30).

Daniel Day Williams has explicated the nature of growth in response to the grace of God.[11] We may say commitment to growth in response to grace is the decision-making propensity of a person. He may decide to keep and hoard what he is given, or he may dispense it as a good and faithful steward. No one who is truly a bestower of grace can forever be miserable, because the "miser" has been removed. He is able, and as an able person he realizes and enjoys the fruits of his labors. But ability is the result of growth. It is not a gift to some, but not to others. Everyone can grow in response to God's grace.

Growth in grace has a beginning, as Williams finds it. The

[11] *God's Grace and Man's Hope* (New York: Harper, 1949), pp. 178-97.

beginning of the new life of the Christian is the birth of faith in the whole man. Faith is born out of the encounter of man with God—the breaking of the shell of self-centeredness and the commitment of the self to the power and goodness of God.

Then, the life of faith is actualized in the process of life. A new way of living commences! The new life is characterized by a new interpretation of the meaning of life, a new devotion to the service of God, and a new participation in the working of God. All of these expressions involve growth in the depth, wisdom, and completeness a person may find in a life of faith.

Yet this growth is not final. New temptation comes at every stage of the Christian experience. In fact, the very release of potential occasioned by the growth tempts the person to test the power which he has gained. Therefore, growth in grace is never away from, but dependent upon, the continuing mercy of God.

Real growth in the strength to love and serve God comes from the developing capacity to discern "all that is true, all that is noble, all that is just and pure, all that is lovable and gracious, whatever is excellent and admirable—fill all thoughts with these things" (Phil. 4:8 NEB). In other words, growth in grace is what persons discover through the expression of Christian wisdom and love. There can be progressive growth in the discernment of what is corrupting and in the appropriation of power to meet the temptation.

Growth in Christian maturity is growth in love for all the values of mortal life, while simultaneously experiencing growth in the capacity to detach our ultimate faith and hope from dependence upon our particular plans, interests, and goals. Whether or not one believes in providence, he must recognize that there is a teleology to his life which is being eventuated. As we have said, God's fulfillment for man is always other than and greater than that which he chooses for himself.

Growth in grace is partially illustrated in the following report from a twenty-seven-year-old woman, married but having no children, regarding a group experience she had just completed. "It was like being born for the first time," she said. "At first I was very silent in the group—although at times I wanted to talk but wouldn't. I was very conscious of the two ministers in the group. They bothered me—I mean, their just being there bothered me—and I felt I just couldn't participate with them sitting there pouncing on everything I said. I had had some real bad experiences with some ministers I have known. Anytime anyone even mentions the word 'church,' I cringe, because I just can't tolerate these church people around where I live. After a while, though, I discovered these ministers were human, and they didn't pounce on me after all. So I began to get the courage to speak out. I had a rugged time, though, because I felt so inferior to everybody that I could hardly talk. Everybody was older than I and they seemed to be able to express themselves better. I suppose if my friend hadn't been there to kind of support me, I would have quit right there. She has always been great to me, and she helped me stick it out. I'm glad because I really grew a lot.

"The time that really sticks out as being important for me was when Glenda [a single woman about the same age] came right out and asked me why it was necessary for me to keep trying to seduce all the men in the group. That really hit hard. I hadn't realized that's what I was doing. She really teed me off, but I was able to say some things to her that I haven't felt free to say to anybody. It almost killed me when she began to cry after I said to her I had the feeling she didn't like it because she wasn't able to do it. I guess we both 'hit home' but we were able to get our feelings out, and then later we both felt warm toward each other. When we embraced at the end of the session, I told her I sure was mad at her for a while, but I thanked her for getting it all out. Well, this is just one of the things that happened. I haven't been too aware of how I am growing, but my husband keeps talking about it—and other people mention it to me. I tell everybody about how this group has helped me to grow and to appreciate more about other people. I feel a lot more grateful for who I am and for what I seem to be able to give to other people. I felt so guilty about just taking in all the time, and not feeling I had anything to offer in return. Now, I am better able to receive from people, because I am beginning to appreciate what I have to give."

This young woman was experiencing growth in grace by acknowledging her own strengths. She was discovering that her gift of herself to the group was not only appreciated but also greatly valued. Also, she was becoming aware that by hiding her strengths she cheated herself as well as other people. She had originally perceived people in the group as "so strong they do not need me and all I can do is take from them." When she learned how grateful they were to receive from her, she came alive. "Just realizing I could give to people in the group has changed everything for me," she said. "I am finding I am not as weak and helpless as I seemed to want everybody to believe. I feel better now that I don't seem to need to present that image any longer." She now had found the grace to accept grace!

One final essential word about the relationship of commitment to creativity: We have not been implying throughout that creativity is merely the accomplishing of creative work. Rather, we mean the creative transformation of the person in the wholeness of his being. A transformed being is a new creation. Creative works are the input and output of a transformed person. In his book *Man's Ultimate Commitment* Henry Nelson Weiman raises the crucial religious question: "What operates in human life with such character and power that it will transform man as he cannot transform himself to save him from the depths of evil and endow him with the greatest good?" [12] The answer to the question contains what is essentially the religious power in a human life.

Wieman sees four distinguishing characteristics in creativity.[13] First, creativity is an expanding of the range and diversity of what one can know, evaluate, and control. We have been discussing the expansion of consciousness. Consciousness is an awareness of data which we appropriate through knowing, evaluating, assimilating, and controlling. Creativity is also the in-

[12] (Carbondale, Ill.: Southern Illinois University Press, 1958), p. 10.
[13] *Ibid.*, p. 4.

creasing of one's ability to understand and appreciate other people, moving across barriers of estrangement and hostility. A phrasing of that theme is given in Bernard Meland's emphasis upon developing "appreciative consciousness," which is a person's sensitive response to the creative character of the world.[14]

Another characteristic of creativity is the exercise of individual freedom. It is the increase of a person's freedom, when freedom means one's ability "to absorb any cause acting on oneself in such a way that consequences express the character and fulfill the purpose of that individual." [15] This was certainly true in the life of Jesus of Nazareth. He responded freely to each situation to fulfill the purpose of his mission. The mark of true personal freedom is the courage to be what one essentially is.

The fourth characteristic has to do primarily with the "capacity for assimilating judgment," which is a theme I have recently developed.[16] Creativity is "increasing the capacity of the individual to integrate into the uniqueness of his own individuality a greater diversity of experiences so that more of all that he encounters becomes a source of enrichment and strength, rather than impoverishing or weakening him." [17] As a person integrates many and diverse experiences, he increases his capacity to integrate further experiences. He is not threatened unduly or humiliated by strange experiences for which his previous understanding does not prepare him. Thus he is open to experiencing and becomes enriched by it.

A physician friend of mine spoke contemptuously of psychology to me (LGC) for many years until he was in an accident and suffered hysterical symptoms which interfered with his ability to perform surgery. Through subsequent counseling he experienced a personal comeback. At the same time, he was

[14] Meland, *Higher Education and the Human Spirit* (Chicago: University of Chicago Press, 1953), pp. 48-78.

[15] Wieman, *Man's Ultimate Commitment*, p. 4.

[16] Colston, *Judgment in Pastoral Counseling*, pp. 36-53.

[17] Wieman, *Man's Ultimate Commitment*, p. 4.

developing a relationship with the hospital chaplain, who had been visiting him regularly. He developed a great appreciation for both the psychologist and the chaplain. In brief, he had gained such freedom and release of spirit that his own creactivity became explosive. He began to express his expanding consciousness in poetry and other writing. Dimensions of himself and others he had once scorned, now to his great satisfaction and fulfillment, he was realizing. Sincere repentance and deep commitment opens a person to the grace of God. Whether or not he responds to that grace depends upon the person's capacity to increase his appreciative awareness. Prodding himself out of the presumably comfortable ruts into which he gets himself, believing he can truly manage his basic anxiety, a person disciplines himself to expand his consciousness and to become differentiating in his awareness. He is now giving himself in personal commitment, which is the appropriate response to the grace of God.

4. Community and History

A man's basic need is for community. He needs the community to complete himself. The mutual strength, encouragement, and support which come from banding together do help people to meet each other's needs. The pooling of creative efforts magnifies the power and effectiveness of the people involved. All are enriched by the cooperative life and work. The extension of labor and services promotes the total welfare of the people who have organized themselves into a community. Each benefits from the other's thought, imagination, and skill. Thus, the community is a total living example of the achievement of truly interdependent behavior required of mature persons.

The community functions as a system. Its structures are planfully instituted. The structures of a community are intended to promote the ebb and flow of its life, implement its culture, sustain the health and welfare of its members, and regulate its economy. At the heart of the system are the appointed and natural leaders of the community (who may or may not be one and the same), who have much to do with setting the pace and affecting the morale of the people whom they serve.

A person incorporates the people of his community. They become a part of him. They are influential in shaping his life. He identifies with certain persons who are significant to him, and they become models for him. The images he receives from them he assimilates and organizes into a concept of himself. He gives this emerging self a unique stamp, but he is always internalizing images of those he admires and respects. This self-image changes in each encounter with another person.

Some of the persons who have become a part of him have had an impact upon him which he has interpreted primarily as negative. Yet they have had as much part in contributing to his self-image as those whom he has liked. They remind him of his gross inability to inspire confidence and trust in everyone he meets! Their distortions offend him. Yet they teach him patience and understanding. They require him to become discerning about the judgments they bring. Also, they challenge him to appropriate interaction in wisdom and love rather than resentment and defensiveness.

Obviously, we are already saying that the community we create both frustrates and fulfills us. It frustrates us when we become embarrassed at the mediocrity of the goals and standards it sets up. Furthermore, values which the community establishes can become rigid and inflexible. Leaders of the community may protect their special interests rather than promote the welfare of members of the whole community. The man who conforms to values set by his community may become provincial and parochial. Another may chafe at the very efforts of such a man to suppress his qualms of conscience regarding the effects of mediocre standards in his community.

An example of such a community is a church which confuses cultural with Christian values. The result is a "culture religion." Cultural values are absolutized. "Religious nationalism" is the act of making one's nation his God. Patriotism or the love

188

of one's country is an expression of loyalty and gratitude for welfare which is sustained by that community. But if love of country or flag—the symbol of that country's integrity and purpose—blinds one to the reality of God's judgment upon all nations, he is practicing religious nationalism. In attitudes and actions which betray justice and righteousness, the "self-righteous" have already desecrated the flag. No one can justify acts of desecration whether in violence to symbols or in feelings and behavior which have already made a mockery of those symbols. Jesus reminded the Pharisees who were incensed at immoral behavior, "If a man looks on a woman with a lustful eye, he has already committed adultery with her in his heart" (Matt. 5:28 NEB). What is in one's heart is crucial. Worship of the state, in any form, has given rise to some of the greatest scourges on mankind—Nazism, Fascism, Communism, are prime examples. The tragedies of history have resulted from idolatrous practices of religious nationalism.

Secular religious materialism is another "culture religion" around which community values may cluster. The person who incorporates such values to the exclusion of all others becomes tragically impoverished. Yet this sounds like a contradiction, for he is devoting his life to making, acquiring, and enjoying material goods! When such acquiring becomes the center of community valuing, *personal* values are inevitably diminished. The clamor for personal significance in societies given over to secular materialism eventually becomes an insistent din. In fact "togetherness," "groupness," "sensitivity training," and other terms describing the yearning for realizing personal consciousness are of the first order of importance.

Still another source of frustration for the church is the persistence of a kind of "practical atheism." A man may profess to be a believer but act as though he were not. While he says he is supporting Christian values, he behaves in such a way as to negate or destroy them. He struggles with the age-old problem of religious man—he confuses his idols with God. He acts as though he does not believe in an ultimate judgment on his proximate values. In fact, the question of his relationship to God in any sense does not concern him *in regard to his behavior.* His profession of faith may be compensatory for his profligate behavior. He pollutes everything, especially his environment, in the name of progress and then seeks to justify his exploitation of people and resources, sometimes invoking the name of the deity to bless his efforts!

The church is not the only community which frustrates man. Political, industrial, and social communities tend to lose perspective and to become caught in frantic efforts to preserve their own structures. They may even destroy the very personal values which they intend to conserve.

Community is also fulfillment. Members strengthen and support each other. They challenge each other to creative endeavor. Expanding awareness of oneself and one's possibilities is generated within a dynamic and vital community. The spiritual function of the church as a community is to incarnate the justice and love of God—to be the "body of Christ" in the world.

Man needs the supporting group. He gives and receives meaning in relation to communities to which he is loyal. He develops his concept of himself as he identifies with and differentiates from other members of the community. Also he gets a notion of who he is and whence he has come. For example, he needs a story of life to tie together the meaning of what he is experiencing with the past. His community supplies interpretations of customs and their derivations. Thus, he learns the whys and wherefores of the behavior of his antecedents. He may choose to break with them, but at least he has some knowledge of what experience has taught regarding meaning and value. Characteristic of man is his concern for meaning, both personal and social. For that reason, he develops an interest in history and philosophy.

His communities, if they are to be sources of fulfillment for him, stimulate a person to achieve both a sense of history and intellectual integrity. The community receiving his loyalty is fulfilling if it is keeping alive in him a tension between his individual sensitivities and the community expectations. Pitfalls in that endeavor are obviously potentially painful. Man is increasingly dependent upon his immediate and larger communities. He asserts himself at the risk of estrangement. Powerful economic and social sanctions may be turned against him. Nevertheless, for the sake of truly creative transformations, such interaction with the community is important, to work changes both in himself and in that community.

We are finding that a sense of history is essential to man's growth: Creativity emerges from historical sensitivity, and responsibility is engendered by an appreciation of history. In an editorial entitled "The Taming of the Individual and the State," Norman Cousins decries the low estate of reason in contemporary life. Along with his concern for the decline of people's interest in reasoning together and the consequent decrease in their ability to do so is his implied alarm at the apparent scorn for history among young people.[18]

A man without a sense of history is a thin, flat, one-dimension man, without the possibility of imaginativeness and creativity which a full-bodied person has. The latter is "full-bodied" because he has incorporated the dimensions of history and is enabled to have an informed perspective upon life and meaning. As Tillich puts the matter:

The center for human consciousness lies in the past. It cannot be sought in the future, for the meaning of the future is determined by it. . . . But the center cannot lie in the present. The present has historical meaning only if it is the point in which are joined the historical fate which is born in the past, and the historical decision which provides the future. In order, however, to have this quality, the present must be able to refer to a center of history, wherein fate and decision have acquired their meaning.[19]

The center of history is a reference point toward which those living in the present turn to interpret who they are and what is their significance. The Jews recalled the exodus from Egypt and the covenant with God on Mt. Sinai. For the American

[18] *Saturday Review*, January 17, 1970, p. 26.
[19] *The Interpretation of History* (New York: Scribner's, 1936), pp. 256-57.

the United States Consititution and the Declaration of Independence are reference points which signify his destiny as a member of a strong and free nation. The meaning of history is interpreted by a referral to significant historical events and the concrete principle which has emerged from them.

Individual persons also have a center of history which has much to do with the way their lives are organized. The appropriation of such meaning constitutes one of the goals of therapy, although some modern therapists see the process as unnecessary, if not indeed wasteful or even a diversionary tactic. Nevertheless, as one is able to deal realistically with who he is by virtue of facing his personal center of history, he is discerningly able to assimilate that history and to incorporate God's judgment in it. One way to know a man is to discover the internal battles he is fighting. Likewise, a man learns about himself as he becomes aware of his historical struggles which have present significance. He becomes more consistent, as he brings together what he has incorporated from his past with his present intentions. Also his energy is released for achieving his creative potential. As one deals with his history, therefore, he gains perspective for revolutionary changes in his present imaging of himself and in his contemporary functioning.

The adventures of love, creativity, forgiveness, reconciliation, commitment, grace, community, and history are the demanding, exciting, and often perilous events dynamic to human experiencing. They are vital to personal and social meaning and fulfillment.

Despite modern outpourings of disillusionment with these concepts and what they reputedly symbolize, we affirm them as living power generating ideas indispensable to Christian faith and life. In whatever concrete form a person experiences what is symbolized by them, he acknowledges and feels a creative breakthrough to a new image of himself and a change in his functioning which verifies such experience for him. He becomes enthusiastic about what he is experiencing and indifferent to how it is labeled.

Norman O. Brown, who wrote a classical study of theological

issues from a psychological point of view, *Life Against Death,* later produced a book, *Love's Body,* which he claimed was to undo what he had done in his earlier work. Brown has lashed out at cribbing structures which hamper and restrict personal freedom. "Permanent revolution, then," he writes prophetically, "and no permanent (reified—visible) structures issuing from contract, commitment, promise, will or will power, which are from the ego. Not voluntarism, but spontaneity, or grace; not the ego but the id." [20] This seems to be an expression of unbridled enthusiasm for chaos, but the healthy note in it is the call to spontaneity and grace, the vital signs of creativity!

If the Christian community is to be the liberating and facilitating community it is intended to be, such spontaneity and grace will be its heartbeat. People will be called out of an automated, insensitized existence to feeling and vibrating with the world around them. They will give expression to an abundant life which has to do with the flow of love rather than material goods. They will be more interested in giving life than suppressing it or controlling it. They will call people out in love, rather than damning them with categories. *Seeing they will see and hearing they will hear.* The robot is an insensitive, efficient machine, which is "programmed" with the "right" words and carefully coded slogans. The person is a sensitive, feeling, caring being whose words come appropriately from his awareness of relatedness.

[20] Quotation in an article on Norman O. Brown by Sam Keen, *Psychology Today,* August, 1970, p. 44.

IX

Caring for Persons: the Christian Vocation

The distinction between a robot and a man hinges upon sensitivity. Caring for persons makes a man a man. The scarecrow in the fantasy *The Wizard of Oz* cries out for a heart, symbolizing the caring which is basically humanizing. He longs for that which would change the perpetual stupid grin on his face to the warm, sensitive visage of one who is able to enter deeply into the feelings of another. He may have the power to put the birds to flight, for his grotesque straw-filled body is designed to repel rather than attract. Of course, the fact that he is able to imagine the joy of having a heart suggests that in some sense he has one already!

1. *Crossing the Barriers and Chasms That Separate*

If we are sensitive to the persons around us, we become aware of deep separation. We may even prefer it that way. We decry any form of bondage as an affront to our dignity as persons. If we cannot be free to go our separate ways, then let us fight and die for the right to be independent. We count no value higher than this essential right to be free from restraint, to decide for ourselves who we will be and where we will go to pursue our separate course of life. Is this not my highest good to be myself and live for myself? So we separate to have it my way.

194

Yet, we are not so fulfilled in our separate life as we had expected to be. To live for oneself is a terribly lonely life. I may demand to be left alone so that I can just be myself. "To thyself be enough," as Peer Gynt said. But then I find I am not enough for myself. I am a fragment of life cut off from my roots, separate as a cut flower without the nourishing vitality of intimate relationships. Life has many assorted pains, but what is more acute than to be empty and cut off from life? To exist in that way is a living death.

The acute feeling of separation has many dimensions, some in the external world and others in the internal world. In the outer world we are separated by boundaries that limit our space and freedom. It is our historic destiny to explore the unknown and conquer the vastness of space by climbing every mountain, crossing every ocean, and surpassing every frontier, even to land on the moon. But we close ourselves in and keep others out by the barriers we erect and the chasms we set between us. The Berlin Wall, like the great wall of ancient China, is a fearful defense to keep enemies out and a frantic effort to close people within our side. Walking in the open fields of the Austrian Alps, we were suddenly stopped by an armed soldier pointing his gun at us from a watchtower at the Hungarian border. "Oh," we said, "this is the Iron Curtain," as we saw the barbed-wire entanglement blocking the frontier.

The inner world reflects and creates the separations of the outer world. Every child learns the sharp difference between "we" and "they." Lines of separation are already drawn by the family into which we are born, and we are conditioned to feel the invisible yet divisive barriers between the ingroup and the outgroup. The family gives us a name and a home. Our identity is shaped and defined by rings of concentric circles that hold us within their walls and identify our position in the world. These separations are reinforced by the expectations of others who claim each of us on their side as one of them. And so within our personalities, barriers form to keep others out and hold them at a distance as strangers and enemies.

In these ways we suffer the pain of estrangement. We are

caught in a web of confining circles as potent and charged as powerful electric wires. Holding back from these social boundaries, we seem to be safe, but crossing the lines of social taboo is "rushing into the wire" to receive the punishing shock of highly charged anger and fear. By constant reminders of social pressure, we are conditioned to view the outsiders with alarm and the insiders with submission to their code. These charged emotions clutch at our throats in acute anxiety and dread at the breaking of taboos.

Programmed in this way to feel the horror of separation, we usually react as "good" members of the loyal group to uphold the taboo and prejudice. We continue to charge and recharge the lines of separation by suspicion of the outsider and fear of the enemy. How can we care for them as persons when they are stamped and labeled as things which are against us and not our kind? We dehumanize the outsiders by epithets and slur names charged with distaste, or ridicule, anger, and rejection. Not seeing them as fully human like ourselves, we reduce them to abstract labels and lump them in a dump heap of worthless and dangerous objects. Or we enslave and exploit them or segregate and ghettoize them, resist and exclude them.

Consequently, our life space as well as theirs is reduced by the barriers that close us in. Building walls to keep others out, we put ourselves in a prison behind these walls. We even raise walls within walls to protect ourselves from others and hold a safe distance from them by retreat into a private world, where we can close the door of our little room and put up signs, "Keep Out—No Trespassing." The modern family is shrinking in life space until each person tends to wall himself in against every other person. Husband and wife may seek at first to be open, but feeling the pain of exposure and the sharp edge of differences, they come to resist and withdraw in anger or protection behind inner defenses. Parent and child respond at first to the warm closeness of the babe in arms nourished by loving care, but then come toilet training and the endless series of disapprovals and coercions that embitter the flavor of these relationships to create divisions of separation and enmity between them.

In our study of personality and Christian faith we must ask how Christians seek to resolve these conflicts and separations. There are many ways of defining a Christian. In historical perspective we begin with Jesus. Can we agree that a Christian is one who responds to the call to follow Jesus? If so, a Christian seeks to understand the mission of Jesus as shown in his life and work. He was concerned for persons in all conditions, and ministered to them in healing, reconciling love. The Christian vocation is caring for persons in the truth and dynamic of such love.

Separations do appear in the Christian way of life. They are not to be denied, but recognized as a human condition to be healed by accepting and forgiving love. The enemy is not to be resisted or excluded, but accepted as one of us. The poor are not to be ignored, but fed and clothed. Children are not to be pushed aside, but given a welcome place of honor. Sinners and criminals are not to be punished by harsh condemnation, but reborn as new beings in forgiving love. The ill are not to be neglected or put away, but drawn to us in loving care. The outcasts are not to be driven away and excluded, but welcomed as equal in value to ourselves. Those who fail and drop out are to be sought and invited into a new community of mutual respect and love.

What does it mean to live in a Christian family today? How are the Christian families in our time working out their relationships at home? In our changing world there are mounting stresses in family life. In the scattering interests and concerns of a mobile society it is not easy to be a family. As we move into the 1970s, many families appear to be cracking at the seams of the generation gap or breaking apart in divorce and separation.

A recent poll shows a painful estrangement between the older and younger generations in their attitudes toward morals and values. Lou Harris & Associates surveyed a cross section of 4,047 Americans to see how they view the present scene in which we are all involved. The social issues surveyed reveal a polarizing response of conflict between persons age 16-20 and those over 50.

Harris Poll of Attitudes and Life Styles
of 4,047 Americans Sampled in 1969 [1]

Attitudes	Age Group 16-20	Age Group Over 50
1. Tastes of the young in music and movies do more good than harm.	56%	15%
2. Books should be censored.	20	55
3. Withdrawal from Vietnam is too slow.	44	20
4. We should build up defenses and let the world take care of itself.	30	57
5. Black demands are justified.	48	31
6. I cannot understand a lot of what is going on in books, music and movies these days.	30	71
7. New styles in hair and dress are signs of moral decay.	36	65
8. I know someone who uses marijuana.	56	5
9. The Establishment is trying to force its ways on the young.	53	20

Sociologists are telling us that young people today live in a youth culture of their own. Young people are not oriented to their parents but to one another in a style of life that displeases and conflicts with the mores and attitudes of the parents. The parents' goals of hard work, success, and material gain are not so prized by the young people. They prefer a simpler and self-

---

[1] From *Life* Poll by Louis Harris, January 9, 1970. © Time Inc.

made happiness, where each does his own thing without the uptight pressures and tensions of the older generation. Relationships between the sexes are freer and more natural. Feeling is a truer guide than thinking. There is concern for the environment, peace instead of war, the rights of the blacks and the poor, social justice, and personal freedom. They are leaving the church, which they feel is stuffy and remote from life. They are eager for personal religious and mystical experiences that give meaning and vitality, openness and new life.

How are Christian families working through the separations of the present generation gap? Are they crossing the barriers and chasms within the home? Some families are living together in love, but many are driving each other mad. Conscientious Christian parents may be overconcerned, anxious, frustrated, and angry in their efforts to control their young people by argument and stern discipline. Other parents are confused and baffled by the changing morals of our modern world; and not knowing what to do, they turn their backs on the children and avoid confrontation. Other parents feel that moral codes are left behind and take permissive attitudes that "anything goes." Others may be discouraged at the seeming irrelevance of the church and prayer, and call on the police to enforce law and order by strong-arm attack on dissenters; with prisons and penalities, they try to knock some sense into the "foolish" heads of young people.

There are other barriers and chasms in our world today between the poor and the rich, the blacks and the whites, Jews and Gentiles, Catholics and Protestants, civilians and military personnel, labor and management, Democrats and Republicans, have and have-not nations, alliances of so-called Communist nations against the so-called democracies, warring nations and cold-war ideologies. How does Christianity transcend these bitter conflicts to reconcile the estranged, forgive enemies, welcome strangers and minority groups, unify separations, and create a loving community caring for each person?

Such a question is a searchlight probing our hearts and hidden desires, our evasions and excuses, to see what our Christian vocation means in this world of conflict and smoldering hatreds. Are we and our Christian friends and enemies really caring for persons on the other side of these walls and chasms? When there are decisions to give or withhold and to act or hide in the crowd, what is manifest in the daily life and the crucial struggles of our time? Do we really care for the stranger and love the enemy enough to share his sorrow and respond to his needs and aspirations?

Christians are likely to regard themselves as loving and compassionate, ready and willing to go out of their way to help other persons. We may know some Christians who respond generously to human need in this way, but is it true of the majority of Christian people today? There is evidence from a number of surveys that churchgoers in our time are more bigoted than those who are not going to church, and that Christians who value salvation highly are less compassionate and less concerned for social justice.

In April, 1969, a nationwide survey was conducted [2] of the value systems of over 1,000 adult Americans ranging in age from 21 to 80, representing a sample of all ages, social classes, and parts of the country. Two values, *salvation* and *forgiving,* stand out above all others as the most distinctly Christian. Included in the survey was a question: "When you heard the news of the assassination of Dr. Martin Luther King, Jr., which one of these was your strongest reaction: (1) anger, (2) sadness, (3) shame, (4) fear, (5) he brought it on himself?" About a third of the respondents said that Dr. King had *brought it on himself,* and another 10 percent reported *fear* as their main response. These responses of 43 percent on items (4) and (5) indicate less social compassion. And they are the persons who ranked highest on *salvation* as their goal.

In other questions the respondents were asked whether this assassination made them "think about the many tragic things that have happened to Negroes." Those who placed a high value on *salvation* were insensitive to such feelings—"It never oc-

[2] Milton Rokeach, "Faith, Hope and Bigotry," *Psychology Today,* April, 1970, pp. 33-37, 58.

curred to me." They also opposed open occupancy and fair-employment laws, desegregation in education, interracial dating and intermarriage. They were unsympathetic to providing a college education, medical and dental care for the poor. They did not favor the church taking part in social and political affairs. There are two primary biblical sources for Christian values: the "thou-shalt-nots" of the Ten Commandments and the "thou-shalts" of the Sermon on the Mount. Evidently the church is more effective in teaching what not to do than what we ought to do.

In 1968 a survey was conducted by a stratified random sample of two thirds of the Protestant ministers in California. A total of 1,580 ministers participated.[3] More than a third of the clergymen said that in their entire ministry they had never taken a pulpit stand on a political issue. A five-point Doctrine Index was used on which each respondent placed himself between the modernist and the traditionalist views. Two thirds of the ministers (68 percent) agreed that "clergymen have great potential to influence the political and social beliefs of their parishioners." But barely half said they frequently discuss public affairs with members of their congregation. And those who gave a sermon during the previous year on socially relevant subjects polarized on the Doctrine Index as follows:

Percentage of 1,580 California Protestant Ministers
Who Gave a Sermon During the Previous Year
Dealing Mainly with These Ethical Issues

Issues	Modernists	Traditionalists	Average
Racial Problems	78%	25%	45%
World Poverty	52	18	28
National Poverty	68	12	22
Crime and Juvenile Delinquency	30	24	20
Sexual Conduct	15	18	16

[3] Rodney Stark, Bruce D. Foster, Charles Y. Glock, and Harold Quinley, "Sounds of Silence," *Psychology Today*, April, 1970, pp. 38-41, 60-61.

Issues	Modernists	Traditionalists	Average
The UN and World Peace	33	6	16
The Use of Drugs	26	16	14
Alcoholism	19	17	14
Capital Punishment	19	4	8
Black Power	22	3	7
The Conduct of Public Officials	15	5	5
Birth Control	19	1	3
Abortion Laws	19	1	2

Reprinted from *Psychology Today* magazine, April, 1970, © Communications/Research/Machines/Inc.

The previous year (April, 1967 to April, 1968) was one of the most agonizing years in American history, with riots in cities, the peace campaign of McCarthy, and the withdrawal of Lyndon Johnson from politics in an effort to negotiate peace. The Middle East was torn by a war with no peace. Biafrans starved and Martin Luther King, Jr. was assassinated. Why were the Protestant ministers so silent on the major social ethical issues at such a time? Only 8 percent of all the ministers believed that "most of my congregation would approve if I gave a sermon on a controversial political and social topic." And when asked for their own opinion, the sharp contrast in theological position was most evident. Here we find that 75 percent of the modernists declare they "personally would strongly approve of a clergyman who gives a sermon on a controversial political or social topic"; while only 12 percent of the traditionalists would approve.

Who can overlook the importance of theology in the behavior of Christian laymen and ministers? Every person lives by what he believes and acts according to the goals he holds before him. What is it in the doctrinal commitment of the conservative clergy that causes them to remain silent? They were asked directly what they thought was the function and mission of the church. Two conflicting views of the Christian mission stood out in bold relief: other-worldly and this-worldly.

The traditionalists see individual salvation as the solution to worldly problems. Clergymen who hold this view concentrate on conversion of the individual and ignore social and political reforms. They see this life as merely a testing time for eternity in heaven. The world is outside and out of bounds, not our business but a diversion from the main business of personal purity to qualify for heaven. "Where will you spend eternity?" is the real issue.

The modernists uphold a more this-worldly goal for the Christian church. We are called to minister to the world around us. God is at work in the world where people are in distress and urgent need. As Jesus went into the world to heal the sick, feed the hungry, forgive the sinner, and care for the poor, he called his disciples into the world with him: Love your enemies, bless them that curse you, do good to them that hate you, pray for them that despitefully use you. He that would be greatest among you, let him be the servant of all. Wash the feet of others as I have washed your feet. Love others as I have loved you, even the least of these are my brothers. Go into all the world and I will be with you.

If Christians are called into the world where Christ is incarnate, is this not where we are to serve?

2. Listening More Deeply to Persons

The fact of the matter is we cannot cross the barriers and chasms that separate us until we listen more deeply to persons. Otherwise, we talk at each other instead of to each other. I make sounds emitting from an isolated me to hear myself talk, or keep silent so you will not hear me. The chatter you hear from me is not true communication, but a jamming of the air waves. The sounding-off I hear from you may be intended for me and actually beat upon my ear drums. But each of us is engaged in monologue, and neither of us is listening enough to share in the deeper interchange of honest dialogue.

You know how a deaf person is lost by not hearing what the other person says. He keeps up the appearance of conversation by talking on brightly, wittily, or engagingly as if he heard you. But actually he is not with you and misses the point of what you were saying. When I am absentminded and thinking of something else, my inattention is the same as deafness, for I am not really listening. I do not care enough about you, or what you are saying, to give you my whole attention. In other words, I turn you off, since I do not want to hear you and do not intend to listen. And you stop talking when you know I am not listening, for what's the use? My barrage of words is just as much a barrier as your silence. And neither of us is hearing the other because we do not care enough to listen more deeply.

Even when we want to hear each other, we may be blocked and misled by our perceptions. A simple conversation between you and me involves at least six persons. There is (1) the one I perceive myself to be, and (2) the one I perceive you to be. Then there is (3) the one you perceive yourself to be, and (4) the one you perceive me to be. (5) But I may not know the person you really are, and (6) you may not know the person I really am. All these perceptions are formed by our previous expectations and experiences with other persons who affected us favorably or unfavorably, and further, by our present interests and concerns of the future. What you mean to me is a very complicated process, and what you see in me is a whole constellation of associations and memories, intentions and feelings.

If we are to accept and understand each other, we must go beyond the unreal images and stereotypes which we project upon the other. We must care enough for the person to listen more deeply, to let him be what he is, and accept him as he is, however surprising or painful the experience may be. This is not easy, for I am as complex and mysterious to you as you are to me. We have learned to be inattentive to the deeper center of persons, and we are not ready to be so involved.

Surface impressions are more visible and audible; they flash upon us and shout at us. So we are caught up in a superficial network of distant relationships that keep us from knowing each other. We are overimpressed by the color of the skin, the style of hair and clothing, the posture and gait, the manner of speaking and presenting ourselves to each other. Much of this is cover-up and evasion, or bluff and acting out a role which we think others expect of us. So we play our games without even knowing who we are.

How does a black man listen to a white man? And how does a white man listen to a black man? Through a haze of color screening as thick as jelly projected from a crisscross network of lifelong associations and culture conditioning. It is over one hundred years since the Emancipation Proclamation and the legal freeing of the slaves. But, as Lincoln said, we cannot escape history. From the beginning of our history as a nation to the present hour, this fair land has been polluted by the residues of human slavery. Africans were enslaved by the greed of white men to exploit their labor and degrade their manhood and womanhood. Black children are born into a culture of white supremacy where they are denied equality and taught to feel ugly, stupid, and inferior. They learn that no matter how hard they work or how capable they may be, the ghetto is their world and they cannot get ahead or rise to open mutuality and equality. They learn from their fathers how dangerous it is to assert the strength of their manhood when they are expected to be dependent and servile. They learn from their mothers it is not safe to be a woman, however chaste and modest you may be.

How, then, can a black person listen to a white person? Knowing how dangerous it is in a white world to stand up for black rights, he may take a deferential approach as if he were a slave bowing before a master. In this situation he listens to the oppressor with anger that may be hidden but is a deep and smoldering volcano within. Knowing that he is not accepted as a black child, he may learn that "white is right" and succeed only by emulating the white norm. Then, seeing that no matter how much he learns, his future is limited by the exclusion and downward pressure of white racism, he drops out of school and sees no point in striving for the impossible dream. Restricted on every hand by unyielding race prejudice and goaded by white oppressors, he will listen hopelessly in a mood of despair and rage.

An educated black woman had worked in an integrated setting for fifteen years. Compliant and deferential, she had earned promotion and pay increases by hard work and excellence. At no time had she been involved in black activism, and her only participation in the movement had been a yearly contribution to the NAACP. During a lull in the racial turmoil she sought psychiatric treatment. She explained that she had lately become alarmed at waves of rage that swept over her as she talked to white people or at times even as she looked at them. In view of her past history of compliance and passivity, she felt that something was wrong with her. If her controls slipped she might embarrass herself or lose her job.

A black man, a professional, had been a "nice guy" all his life. He was a hard-working, non-militant who avoided discussions of race with his white colleagues. He smiled if their comments were harsh and remained unresponsive to racist statements. Lately he has experienced almost uncontrollable anger toward his white co-workers, and although he still manages to keep his feelings to himself, he confides that black and whites have been lying to each other. There is hatred and violence between them and he feels trapped. He too fears for himself if his controls should slip.[4]

How does a white man listen to a black man? First, by knowing that our viewpoint is saturated in the poison of white racism that has colored and distorted our perceptions since the first slave was brought in chains to America. Second, by seeing how we are misguided by surface appearances like skin color and external arrangements of segregation and injustice, to imagine we are more different than we are. And third, by sensitivity to the profound hurt and despair and anger that our white superiority complex has driven into their souls, most of which we have not cared enough about to understand.

Speaking for myself (PEJ), I once thought I had been emancipated from white racism, even though I enjoyed the

[4] William H. Grier and Price M. Cobbs, *Black Rage* (New York: Basic Books, Inc., Publishers, 1968), p. 207. This perceptive study by two black psychiatrists at University of California Medical Center, San Francisco, well repays reading.

privileges of a favored position in our world of poverty and injustice. I sincerely felt we were brothers, and I wanted to do my best to bridge the chasm, remove the barriers, and work for equal opportunity in all areas of life. Then, one evening after crossing the street to mail a letter, I was suddenly seized from behind, beaten and robbed by two black men. As the beating mounted in fury, I struggled in vain to shake them off and be free. They completely overpowered me with a strength greater than my own. There could be no doubt who was superior then. I had to submit in helpless anguish and despair.

For the first time in my life, I began to understand how it feels to be a black person. Nothing I had learned from all I had read nor from all the words I had exchanged in many wonderful hours with my black friends reached me as deeply as this beating. My shield of righteousness was broken, and my safe defenses cracked into sharp fragments of inescapable, unbearable pain. These were body blows falling upon me in a torrent of unleashed fury. In these uncounted and interminable moments I and they shared one experience of violent suffering, which for them reflected years of hopeless anguish, and for me shattered years of living apart.

Then followed long days and nights of agony, during which I listened as never before. The intolerable pain of my bruised body was overtaken by the even greater pain of soul searching. What were my black neighbors saying to me in this violent encounter? Why did they attack me in such overwhelming fury? I saw them by the mailbox, where they asked me, "What time is it?" What time indeed? Much too late to repent of white supremacy and accept them as equals in one world. They followed me across the street, talking to each other in words I did not comprehend. The talking ceased, and I was caught in a vicelike grip with a hand covering my mouth. How feeble and futile are words when engaged in such a furious struggle packed with three hundred years of cruelty and repression. Under the crushing blows of black fists, I heard the body language and knew why it was my turn to be beaten until I was limp and helpless. I was "Whitey" bearing the white man's burden of all the hurt that white men have given black men.

> This dismal tone of depression and hopelessness . . . stirs these feelings . . . tasted by black people in America.
>
> The horror carries the endorsement of centuries and the entire life span of a nation. It is a way of life which reaches back to the beginnings of recorded time. And all the bestiality, wherever it occurs and however long it has been happening, is narrowed, focused, and refined to shine into a black child's eyes when first he views his world. All that has ever happened to black men and women he sees in the victims closest to him, his parents.
>
> A life is an eternity and throughout all that eternity a black child has breathed the foul air of cruelty. He has grown up to find that his spirit was crushed before he knew there was need of it. His ambitions, even in their forming, showed him to have set his hand against his own. This is the desolation of black life in America.
>
> Depression and grief are hatred turned on the self. It is instructive to pursue the relevance of this truth to the condition of black Americans. . . .
>
> As grief lifts and the sufferer moves toward health, the hatred he has turned on himself is redirected toward his tormenters, and the fury of his attack on the one who caused him pain is in direct proportion to the depth of his grief. When the mourner lashes out in anger, it is a relief to those who love him, for they know he has now returned to health.[5]

All this comes home to me in a new way since I was beaten into submission. My tormenters have become my teachers. They have introduced me into their fellowship of pain. Now I know a little bit, an infinitesimal hint of what they suffer. I feel more deeply what they feel, and enter vicariously into their anguish. The color line which separates us has brought us together in this revealing encounter. The Fellowship of Pain, as Albert Schweitzer says, is a holy order including all who suffer. To suffer pain is to join with others who suffer at the deeper levels of intense feeling, to know our common sorrow, and discover our responsibility to care for one another." To respond to this revelation, he left his favored position in Europe and

[5] *Ibid.*, pp. 208-10.

entered medical training, to dwell among the Africans in Lambaréné to ease their suffering.

It is evident that the Christian vocation of Schweitzer was caring for persons. But with all the Christians in the world, why are there so few Schweitzers? Why is Sunday morning the most segregated hour of the week? How do Christian church members care for their black brothers and sisters? This question is now openly asked of white churches by James Forman in presenting the Black Manifesto. Yet instead of hearing this as a cry for help, many churchmen heard it as an unwarranted attack upon our "innocent" righteousness. There are church leaders who do hear this as an appeal "to help us help ourselves," and who contribute to black churchmen for a program of economic self-improvement. But many white Christians respond in anger: "This is preposterous to interrupt our worship. What have we to do with you?"

In such a time of confusion and mutual hostility, it is not easy to listen to persons and hear the profound anguish of all this pain. Yet there is no other way to know each other but to be open and honest in our communications. Too long we have been hiding from each other and holding up barriers to shield our eyes from the bitter truth. It is natural to prefer comfort to agony, hoping we are not to blame, and to fabricate excuses and fictions to protect our pride. We can now be thankful that the silence is broken by sharper cries, that voices once muffled and feelings long repressed are shouting and calling to be heard.

Is it so strange that slavery should enslave the masters as well as the slaves? If the shackles are not yet broken, how can the sight and hearing of the oppressors be restored? Are we not all bound together in these unhappy and constricting relationships? When we are interrelated, must we not live or die together? Even if we look the other way and avoid encounter, we are on a collision course, and in one way or another we must hear and accept black and white in one common life. If we cling fanatically to labels and stereotypes, we only blind our eyes. And if we listen to "my rights" against yours, we only defeat and destroy ourselves.

Are we not one race of human persons who contribute to each other the joy and vitality of our unique potentialities? Yet we have not seen each other with open eyes or heard each other with open ears. We have downgraded one and upgraded another in a relentless struggle for power and false superiority. In such ways we diminish ourselves by reducing our human stature and shrinking our unrealized potentiality. The time has come to see each other more honestly and hear each other more distinctly, as persons calling forth the greater creativity we have not yet been willing to share.

What it all comes down to in the final analysis is this. If we are self-centered, we do not really hear each other. For I am so busy listening for what pleases and displeases me, I have no time to listen to what concerns you. Bonhoeffer identified Jesus as "the man for others." If our Christian vocation is for others, we are devoted to others. And if there is any healing power in the good news of Jesus, should this not set us free from the prison of a self-centered life? It is a Christian's hope to find himself free of selfish egocentricity, that he may expand in loving concern toward others. Growing or leaping toward such maturity is freeing us to care for persons. And that in reality is our best hope of finding each other in a community of accepting and forgiving love.

3. Dynamic Responsiveness in a Small Group

Listening more deeply to persons frees us for participation in groups which make up the community of accepting and forgiving love. However, just listening, which sounds passive (although listening is an active form of participation in a happening), is not enough. An active response is required. The power is in the *interaction*, in which what we have received from the other is accepted, and what we give of ourselves in return is received.

The popularity of small groups has increased over the past

few years. Why is this phenomenon occurring? Clyde Reid is of the opinion that "people everywhere are hungry for depth relationships. They need such relationships to give them a point of security and belonging in a world of rapid change and mass society. Small groups also can supply the deep needs of human beings for love and acceptance that are so impossible to find in a crowd of a hundred or a thousand." [6]

We cannot check out the communications of "a hundred or a thousand." We are unable to learn what possible personal significance we have even to one or more of that multitude. Perhaps being a part of a large crowd at a trememdously impressive event satisfies our need to be a part of greatness, but what about our need for intimacy? How can we learn whether or not we can truly relate to others in depth, unless we interact with them in a group small enough to allow depth encounters? What of our tremendous potential for growth? Is it enough to be impressed by the great talents of another and simply be satisfied to participate vicariously in his achievements? Is there not a nagging suspicion that there are talents within us? But how can the talents of everyone be recognized in a large group? These are some of the questions which impel us to seek out small groups which offer us opportunities for growth.

There is a great power potential in a small group. Henry Nelson Wieman regards the small group as the possible source for the creative event. "Jesus engaged in intercommunication with a little group of disciples with such depth and potency that the organization of their several personalities was broken down and they were remade. They became new men, and the thought and feeling of each got across to the others." [7] We are regarding this as the prototype for a dynamic and creative small group. The group leader is an enabler or catalyst for the group. He helps to create the climate and set the group in motion. However, his ability to relate to others in depth and

---

[6] Clyde Reid, *Groups Alive* (New York: Harper. 1969), p. 16.
[7] *The Source of Human Good* (Chicago: University of Chicago Press, 1946), p. 39.

power sets the mode and the style for the life of the group. This is true whether the person is the designated or the emergent leader of the group. Ideally, members of the group take turns giving leadership to the group. Out of such interaction emerges "a miraculous mutual awareness and responsiveness to the needs and interests of one another." [8]

The small group becomes a representation of a family to the person. The sibling rivalries, jealousies, desires for acceptance, bids for attention from other members, and other actions typical of family interactions are all there. The assurances we need from our families for our own growth are sought similarly from members of the group. We wish to test out and feel the strength of members of the group (as we do with parents and other members of our families), thus gaining satisfaction that we, too, have strength and power.

Whitaker and Lieberman, discussing psychotherapy through the group powers, indicate the basic purpose of the member of a therapeutic group is to become assured regarding the strength and competence of the therapist. In gaining the acceptance of the strong and competent therapist, he increases his own self-esteem immeasurably. Therefore, the basic dynamics of the therapeutic group are: (1) the operation of a "disturbing motive" (the wish to be unique and singled out by the therapists for special gratification). This is opposed by: (2) a "reactive motive" (the fear of disapproval and retaliation by therapists). The members of the group are then working toward: (3) "a solution" (which is that the needs of all are to be served and fulfilled).[9] The mutual satisfaction which the one being served and the one performing the service gains is of eye-opening gratification to the participants. Each discovers strengths in himself and the other of which he was previously unaware. The community achieved in the process of working cooperatively for a solution is the community which is fulfilling, because it emerges out of the people who are thus

[8] *Ibid.*, p. 40.

[9] Dorothy Stock Whitaker and Morton A. Lieberman, *Psychotherapy Through the Group Process* (New York: Atherton Press, 1964), p. 19.

banded together. They are incorporated and the group matures as a person does—through stages of growth and development.

Reid has aptly characterized the stages in a group's growth as follows. When a small group is given a measure of freedom, they move in relation to the authority of the leader: (1) from dependence upon the designated leader, (2) through a period of resistance to the freedom offered them, (3) through adolescent rebellion, through a period of celebration of the victory of the rebellion and independence, (4) to a time of responsible interdependent interaction with original leader authority. A crisis may force the group to reactivate the cycle.[10] If people are given the freedom to work through these stages of growth in a small group, they experience the group as releasing them from attitudes and feelings inhibitory to their growth.

An illustration of the fears and expectations of a person joining a small group is seen in the following quote from John Mann's book *Encounter*, a report of a weekend with intimate strangers:

[The group leader is asking questions of members of the group as the first session begins. The parenthetical material is that of random thoughts of one participant as she responds internally to what is going on.]

"What is it that you would like to achieve or experience while you are here? I am not asking you to say out loud. Just come to a definite conclusion for yourself."

(A minute of deep silence ensues. I am thinking. Nothing seems to come. What am I supposed to want? It would be easier if it were going to be made public. I have a pretty good idea what he wants me to want. What is the leader's name anyway? Richard, I wonder what people call him. . . . But what do I want? It would be nice to feel happy, but that doesn't seem adequate. . . . I would like to face something about myself. . . . But what . . . I don't know. That sounds so therapeutic. . . . I guess what I would really like to know, what I would really like to sense is the nature of my capacities! What I could become.)

"All right. Now I give you another task. . . . Decide for yourself what you are most afraid might happen to you during the weekend.

[10] *Groups Alive*, p. 62.

Again keep it to yourself. But decide on something definite and real."

(The silence this time is different. It has an ominous quality. I am afraid that everyone will suddenly start staring at me accusingly. I am afraid people will find out that I am just curious and get angry at me. No, no that is all trivial. I am afraid of being found out. I guess that is it. But about what? By whom? I don't know. But that is the feeling. I have had it before.[11]

At first blush, one might get the impression she was experiencing guilt feelings. Yet the whole impact of her feelings is a profound fear of being found impotent, unable to cope with the group.

Although a grave injustice is done to the sometimes terribly painful, sometimes wonderfully exciting intermediate process by skipping to the end, nevertheless, we will listen to Marcia reporting her feelings during the last session of the group:

(I feel cozy and complete. . . . If I have a momentary fear, I can visualize myself talking about it and it goes away. . . . I am protected. . . . I am naked.

(I hurt inside. I have been bruised. Is it the after effects of surgery or just a blow? I can't tell. . . . I am happy to be alive. . . . I am grateful to be here. . . . I am so grateful to feel that there is really a chance for me. . . .

(Will it last? It can't, I suppose, and I can't try to keep it. . . . Where has it all gone—the tensions, the suspicion, the confessions? Has the earth absorbed them? I cannot think. . . . I am here. . . . The sun is touching me . . . going through me. . . .

(My body is quiet. My mind is a whisper. . . . My personality is almost transparent. . . . Nature is reflected in me. . . . My sensations are surprises coming from the outside . . . from a mysterious place . . . on the first day . . . on the last one . . . unknown . . . unless it reveals itself. . . .

(Mother, I can see you now. . . . I am close to you. . . . Your daughter whom you left behind so reluctantly . . . you need not be afraid . . . . I bless you for giving me the chance to be here. . . . I was always indifferent before. Life is such a mean and grubby struggle. . . . It hasn't changed. . . . But there is a shining, throbbing jewel at the center that alters everything. . . . Do you

[11] John Mann, *Encounter* (New York: Grossman Publishers, 1969), pp. 3-4.

know what I am talking about? Do you still exist? Do you remember me?)[12]

Marcia is now open to an interdependent relationship with her deceased mother. She carries on the encounter dialogically in her imagination and feels a warmth toward her mother and a depth of appreciation she had never previously acknowledged.

We tie the beginning and end points of Marcia's reporting of her experiences with the group, not to obscure the process itself, but to show the dramatic, creative transformation which occurred.

Her interaction with members of the group has enabled Marcia to realize the significance of a dynamic organization of her life around a center of meaning and purpose. She affirms that reality almost wistfully. However obliquely she refers to a "shining, throbbing jewel at the center that alters everything," she has actually realized the power of divine love and acceptance. Her discovery generates the wish in her to share the joy of the reality she is experiencing with her deceased mother, whom she imagines, somehow, would understand what has happened to her. More than that, however, she spontaneously expresses her gratitude for her birth—for the "chance to be here." She is now blessing her existence rather than being apathetic, as she confessed she had previously been.

We have increasingly witnessed similar transformations among members of small groups with whom we have worked. They have been astonished at the truth which breaks upon them and releases them from the egocentric devices which have locked them up. They are invariably amazed at the increase in their capacity for discernment and at their own growth in spirit.

The small group process is not some kind of magic cure-all. Dynamic interaction requires disciplined structuring as well as perceptive and sensitive responsiveness. People do not just meet and begin opening up to each other. Genuine trust must be established and demonstrated. As much willingness to be exposed as to expose others must be evident. The basic prin-

[12] *Ibid*, pp. 185-86.

ciple: Working to help the other realize personal fulfillment in direct measure contributes to one's own fulfillment, then becomes the guiding factor.

Honest and open encounter out of positive regard for the other is participation in God's active work of redeeming love in the world. Small groups provide the intimate setting wherein such participation can be activated among the people. The persons are supported and enriched by the community they create. Of course that kind of differentiation of a community into small groups has its dangers. Shared feelings, attitudes, and experiences, create special kinds of relationships which "outsiders" do not know nor, perhaps, even understand. Exclusiveness may be mutually felt or distortedly perceived by those outside. Yet the degree of intimacy achieved by the small group is necessary to foster the creative potential of each person involved. There is literally no comparable social organization which will permit or provoke individual persons to realize their possibilities. Jesus' choice of twelve disciples to become his apostles was surely not a historical accident, but a design of inherent wisdom. For the creative energy of vitally interacting persons in small groups sets in motion the systems which actualize God's activity in the world. God's judgment and mercy, flowing from his love and acceptance, are realized in the small groups wherein responsiveness to God's love can be implemented in effective relationships.

What is the appropriate context of the small group? We are saying it is *koinonia*, or the gathering of people who are participating in God's redeeming action in the world. Should the members of the small group be conscious of the nature of their participation? We think so. The act of celebrating their common life and work dramatizes and brings into focus their recognition of God's saving grace working in and among them. Such celebration and thanksgiving is an act of gratitude essential to any relationship, especially to God whose grace and acceptance address us in the midst of our needs. Our responsiveness in small groups is in itself an expression of gratitude and a cause for celebration!

A group is continually struggling for identity. We do not find identity in one-dimensional relationships. The appropriate context of the group, therefore, is the community which is always defining itself—seeking continually to be conscious of its history and destiny in relation to God.

4. Koinonia *as the Heart of a Christian Community*

A Christian community receives its energy and vitality from those whom tradition has called "redeemed souls." These are the people of God, whom Harvey Cox designates as those "who participate in God's action in the world." *Koinonia* is the "visible demonstration of what the church is saying in its *kerygma* and pointing to in its *diakonia*." [13] It is the concrete representation of hope. The vigorous action of those who are confidently expecting the new regime of God has always been characteristic of those who comprise the *koinonia*. They are witnessing to the present reality of God's dynamic activity in the world.

The person who is experiencing *koinonia* does not talk about love and grace in some vague and unfamiliar terms. He is accepting the present reality of that grace and acting appropriately. We cited earlier the story of the woman in the Pharisee's house. She was not protesting her understanding of God's grace; she was demonstrating how that power affected her in her works of care and love. She had the boldness to minister to Jesus' needs not merely from a desire for erotic satisfaction, as the Pharisee probably was implying, but from a heart overflowing with gratitude.

The person who is truly participating in the *koinonia* is not now preoccupied with his safety and security or filled with ego-satisfaction, but is overwhelmed with gratitude in response to forgiveness and acceptance. He does not claim his "righteousness" for himself. He is not convinced he is among the few who own it, but he shares it and demonstrates the redeeming activity of God in the world. He witnesses, not by saying "see

[13] *The Secular City* (New York: Macmillan, 1965), p. 144.

what I've got that you don't have, but by showing "see how I have been transformed by the knowledge that my sins have been forgiven."

Koinonia is achieved in mutual interaction among those who accept the task of proclaiming and showing the world what God's redeeming action in the world really is. The church's message has always been that of proclaiming the coming kingdom, not as a *fait accompli,* but as a continuing realization of a future which is now—but also is not yet.

A hint of such promise was realized by a young woman who was a member of one of our counseling groups.

"When I came into the group, I half-hoped and half-expected that all of my problems would suddenly vanish, and all my fears would be gone. I can't say that happened. But it doesn't seem to matter so much anymore. I still have the same old problems, but now they look different to me. Members of my family say that they notice changes in me which they like. Knowing that I have you [she gestured with a slight swing of her hand toward members of the group] has made all the difference in the world. I didn't realize how much it could mean to me to be a part of a group like this.

"I think part of it is: I was coming at first for what *I* could get out of it. It didn't occur to me that I really had anything to offer anybody else. I guess that's been the problem all along . . . , and it's kept me from doing anything much for anybody. I have found out that you [she looks out toward other members of the group] value me. That's a new feeling for me. It has opened me up to being aware of people around me in a way I have never been. It's kind of exciting and kind of frightening, too [she shudders visibly], but I like the feeling.

"I guess it doesn't seem so suprising to some people that you can find people that you can trust. But it's been an awakening to me.

"I have to admit I was even ashamed of my family background, but with you it doesn't seem important. . . . I mean, that I have felt it was bad and all that. In fact, I am not thinking about that as much as I did. Every time I got into a group, I began to compare myself to the other people and thinking of the ways I could see they were better than me. Right away, I was thinking about my family background and being ashamed and not saying anything . . . and telling myself I was probably better than they were anyway, so why knock myself out about them.

"I even started out that way here. I knew I needed this . . . but I both wanted to be here and I didn't. At the beginning I began to feel awful because some people could express themselves very well and I couldn't at all. Then I began to find out these people were human, too, and we could enjoy each other and trust each other. Then something really happened to me. And, as I said, the family has noticed it, too. At first I found it hard to believe, but now I know you really do care. And I find myself wanting to tell other people what's possible for them. But I keep forgetting. . . . They'd probably think I'm a kook or something.

"Of course, right now that really doesn't bother me too much. Other people can believe what they want. I *know* how I feel now. I know I've got a lot of unfinished business, but I see a little bitty ray of hope. [She fashions her two fingers into a small aperture through which she squints at the other members of the group. The others laugh and she laughs with them]. I like that! [She says this emphatically. She pauses, then speaks quietly.] I just want to say. Thank you. [Her lips tremble and she quickly brushes a tear from the corner of her eye and smiles broadly.]"

She has realized one important dimension of *koinonia*: a common affirmation of hope toward which all are working.

Koinonia is not just a pleasant and sentimental ingathering, but the acting community, demonstrating care and concern for the world. *Koinonia* is risk-taking involvement in the lives of people who are truly "members of each other." "But God has combined the various parts of the body, giving special honor to the humbler parts, so that there might be no sense of division

219

in the body, but that all its organs might feel the same concern for one another. If one organ suffers, they all suffer together. If one flourishes, they all rejoice together." (I Cor. 12:24-26 NEB.) Thus Paul discusses analogically the nature of *koinonia*. The whole body suffers when one member suffers, or flourishes when one member flourishes. The whole community is affected by what happens to one of its members or groups. Oppression of one stigmatizes all. Liberation of one in the same sense frees all.

Expressions of *koinonia* in the world are both signs and living models of the kingdom of God. In the latter regard, as Cox suggests, "they are instances of the coming of the Kingdom, just as Jesus' coming was." [14] They demonstrate what the kingdom of God is now, as it being fulfilled in our midst. They are also signs in the sense of pointing toward the future coming of the kingdom.

Koinonia is thus the visible expression of hope in the world, the indication of the "now" and "not yet" in the coming of the kingdom and of what both are like. "The church is one of the signs, and it points to and supports the other signs. It is wrong to identify the church with the kingdom. Its whole existence is a derivative one, dependent entirely on the prior reality of the kingdom." [15] The church, therefore, is a visible sign of hope in the world, but should point beyond itself to other signs of the kingdom.

Without the dynamic reality of *koinonia*, the person lacks the capacity for true discernment of the signs of hope in the world; consequently, he may lose perspective upon existence and the world. His participation in *koinonia* enables him to gain perspective which, in turn, gives order and organization to his life.

Koinonia really forms around a common affirmation of the *agape* of God at work in the world. Wherever the love of God is being acted upon and witnessed, there is *koinonia*.

[14] *Ibid.*, p. 146.
[15] *Ibid.*, p. 147.

5. Agape *Love as the Healing of Alienation*

We feel the indignation and outrage in the statement of a Negro bishop who calls for a truly united America.

Even as lynching was the Roman holiday sport of nineteenth-century America, killing black Americans promiscuously has been the twentieth-century pastime of our police, whose primary duty is law enforcement and peace.

I'm thinking of the six Negroes killed in Augusta, Georgia, all shot in the back, of the Panthers slain in their beds in Chicago; of the students slain at Jackson State College; of the almost daily news stories of the indiscriminate, ruthless slaying of black Americans by police and civilians, under the guise of "law and order," but actually fulfilling the guidelines of a bitter, white majority, whose vain effort to keep us "in our place" leads them to resort to the policeman's pistol and kangaroo court trials.

The white liberals and the churches have not been conspicuous in the fight for freedom lately. No one questions the demand for an immediate end of the Vietnam war. We ask again why is it that white people always find some issue other than race to which they give their priority attention, the latest of which is pollution and ecology? [16]

We have quoted this rather lengthy statement in its entirety because it states well the nature of the alienation between blacks and whites which has often been seen as evidence of real polarization of the races. Bishop Spottswood's hard-hitting address was a call for national unity even while it witnessed to the alienation which exists.

We cannot deny the intense feelings of antipathy which have developed between blacks and whites. Some view the situation with alarm. Others are not adequately alarmed about its seriousness.

The apparent "white backlash" and "black retreat" has put a definitely "drag chute" effect on efforts toward integration. Thus, efforts to establish one society have been slowed down

[16] From an address delivered June 29, 1970, before the Annual Convention of the National Association for the Advancement of Colored People, Cincinnati, Ohio, by Stephen G. Spottswood, Bishop of the African Methodist Episcopal Zion Church.

considerably, and instead vigorous activity in developing two societies is evident.

However, alienation between the races is not the only evidence of polarization in the society. The so-called generation gap, the women's liberation movement, and the breakdown in marriages are phrases which characterize other areas wherein alienation between persons and groups is being experienced.

Alienation of any kind cannot be overcome in the subtle niceties which really conceal our idolatrous tendencies to use God to support our own absolutized partial perspectives. We must allow God through the operation of *agape* love to break our stubborn hold on what we have formed into cherished idols and be opened up to the expansion of our appreciative consciousness.

Donald Browning has described well the *agape* love of God:

> The God who affirms us and who enters into our lives with unconditioned empathic acceptance does not rob us of our autonomy or stifle our growth toward maturity. The God of the atonement, the God of suffering and weakness of the cross, does not take over the executive functions of our lives; he does not frustrate our attempt to master and direct our own future responsibly.
>
> Instead, this is the God who constitutes the ground of all advance into responsible autonony by being an invariant source of affirmation and love.
>
> All human relationships that facilitate growth operate in analogy to his atoning love for mankind.[17]

The *agape* love of God enables man to enter wisely and discerningly into the task of negotiating his differences and to act on his hunches about what will strengthen and improve his relationships. He is also enabled to become more trusting of his experience and that of others, thus accepting it as a means of growth in grace. He does this only as he acknowledges the *agape* of God which puts together what he has pulled apart in his pride, stubbornness, and resentment. *Agape* love is symbolized in the cross which represents God's agonizing with

[17] *Atonement and Psychotherapy* (Philadelphia: Westminster Press, 1966), pp. 258-59.

the world, signifying the love which overcomes alienation and despair through reconciliation and hope.

6. Faithful Self-giving as the Power of Christian Faith

Carl Rogers was once challenged by Martin Buber in a dialogue to acknowledge that even the way Rogers structured his counseling interviews suggested an inequity in the relationship. This was not a true I-Thou encounter, Buber insisted. Rogers granted that the initial interview may truly be perceived by the client as inequitable. In fact, that was precisely the reason Rogers was there—to help the client overcome that feeling. All he could really do, Rogers said, was to offer himself, without conditions, to the other person. Rogers affirmed this self-giving in "unconditional positive regard" for the other person as a cardinal principle governing him in his therapeutic relationships.

Another psychotherapist, Dr. Sidney S. Jourard, makes a similar affirmation: "Would it be too arbitrary an assumption to propose that people become clients *because they do not disclose themselves in some optimal degree to the people in their life?*" [18] "And it seems to be another empirical fact that *no man can acknowledge his real self to himself (that is, know himself) except as an outcome of disclosing himself to another person.*" [19]

Self-giving, therefore, represents the power which not only prompts the other to reveal himself in responsiveness, but also enables the giver to know himself. Significant aspects of the self remain hidden to others and to oneself until they are brought out in the act of self-giving. The assumption that any person has some kind of prior knowledge of himself is simply not true. He becomes known to others and to himself in his acts of self-disclosure.

Faithful self-giving is significant therapeutically because the process is essential to any creative interpersonal relationship.

[18] *The Transparent Self: Openness, Effectiveness, and Health* (New York: Van Nostrand, 1964), p. 21.
[19] *Ibid.*, p. 5.

Indeed, self-giving is at the heart of all relationships, or a relationship is hardly possible.

The life and ministry of Jesus Christ embodies faithful self-giving. The very ordering of his existence was around this dynamic activity of continual self-disclosure in acts of love and giving. His ministry of healing, freeing people from all kinds of oppression and assuring them of hope, flowed consistently from his concept of himself which he had not preconceived but was forming in dynamic interrelationships with God and man. Those who are "in Christ," to use the term the apostle Paul employed to describe Christians, carry on the ministry of self-giving.

The capacity to "put on" one's neighbor—his joys, his sufferings, his pain, his frustrations, and fulfillments—is at the heart of self-giving.

Faithful self-giving is responsiveness to God's love which is manifest in acts of courage and strength. "I will not forsake you" is the key phrase of assurance which is substantiated in acts of integrity. To stand by the other in the midst of adversity, in the face of rejection, and at the cost of suffering is the measure of self-giving.

The capacity to "put on" one's neighbor—his joys, his sufferings, his pain, his frustrations, and fulfillments—is at the heart of self-giving.

Remarkably, a person will often give of himself to another who has not the good grace to respond to grace until others regard the action as utter foolishness. In such cases, the heart has reasons that reason knows not.

Certainly, the love of God for man, as expressed in the Incarnation, is the "saving power of God for everyone who has faith" (Rom. 1:16 NEB). What the incarnate act of self-giving means is well summarized in Paul's letter to the Philippians: "Let your bearing towards one another arise out of your life in Christ Jesus. For the divine nature was his from the first; yet, he did not think to snatch at equality with God, but made himself nothing, assuming the nature of a slave. Bearing the human likeness revealed in human shape, he humbled himself, and in obedience accepted even death—death on a cross. Therefore, God raised him to the heights and bestowed on him the name above all names, that at the name of Jesus every knee should bow—in heaven, on earth, and in the depths— and every tongue confess, 'Jesus Christ is Lord,' to the glory of God the Father." (Phil. 2:5-11.)

"Snatching at equality with God" is a perennial human propensity. Yet the servant role of the Christian is clearly indicated here and is the model for personal behavior. However, the model is not a "put on" or a copied role, but one of genuine participation in what Thomas Oden has termed God's self-disclosure. Referring to the statement of Jourard which we have already quoted, Oden says: "An adequate theory of therapy must not only understand therapeutic growth as a product of human self-disclosure, but authentic human self-disclosure as a response to the self-disclosure of God in being itself." [20]

Self-disclosure as the power of Christian faith is actualized through an appropriation of the *agape* love of God who is hidden yet revealed. Marcia, the member of the group whose experience we cited earlier, described this reality she discovered as "a shining, throbbing jewel at the center." That is what we are saying: The divine self-disclosure is at the center, not out on the periphery somewhere. In this recognition the person is born again. Nicodemus' problem becomes a key one; recognition of the response to his fundamental question is essential to the solution, "You ought not to be astonished, then, when I tell you that you must be born over again. The wind blows where it wills; you hear the sound of it, but you do not know where it comes from, or where it is going. So with everyone who is born from spirit" (John 3:8 NEB).

Christian faith is empowered by the assurance that God's self-disclosure comes through every expression of caring. This truly is the central vocation. All that is done in the name of Christian faith is essentially related to that vocation, or it is not worthy of the name.

[20] *Kerygma and Counseling* (Philadelphia: Westminster Press, 1967), p. 43.

Caring for persons does not mean just doing something *to* them or *for* them. In fact, the latter may spring more from our own needs than theirs. Caring means doing whatever enables them to realize their strength. We may urge, help, confront, support, or whatever is immediately appropriate and relevant to their particular needs. Thus we encourage persons to become truly interdependent.

One more important thing is required: the action which translates this caring into transforming energy in the communities of the world. This statement may sound contradictory because people get hurt when such action is undertaken. They get hurt when they try to suppress and control, which are not ways of caring for persons. We will examine in the next chapter how action transforms people.

X

Personal and Community Transformation

In the act of caring for persons, a person or community is changed. Calling out another person's strength adds immeasurably to those who extend the caring concern. As one grows all grow. As one is healed all are healed. One act of reconciliation affects positively the whole community.

If caring for persons is genuine, and not a deceitful guise for using or controlling them, a remarkable transformation of everyone concerned occurs. On the other hand, the manipulation of persons for purposes of control reduces them to automatons. In the long run, when the latter happens, the whole community is impoverished. People are limited by the limitations of those who control them. Their rich creative potentialities are choked and stifled. This is especially true in the area of human interaction in a technological society. Created goods are in abundance, but creative transactions are nil because the capacity for trust is diminished.

What is the nature of creative personal transactions? How can they contribute to changes in institutional structures, especially when these structures suppress rather than liberate people affected by them? Can trust be established? What is required to enlarge man's spirit?

Personal tranformations occur as we permit the open flow and differentiation of data from our own fantasy world. Out of such data comes the progressive individuation of science, education, and religion. The poetic, the artistic—in fact, the whole of the aesthetic—possibilities can be realized by every person. Not only talented artists, but every person has a richly furnished fantasy world. To the degree he loses contact with this world, he becomes impoverished. As he draws upon these data, he begins to actualize his potentialities. Man thus fulfills himself as spirit, for the great spiritual genius of man breaks through with every encounter of the depth of his own possibilities and every engagement with the essence of others.

Many churches have become alert to the needs for such expression among their members. Increasingly, art fairs and festivals, or whatever they may be called, are being conducted periodically in a number of churches across the country. Most of them include exhibits of various media of expression, such as painting, sculpture, photography, various crafts (pottery, etc.), poetry, and many others. These efforts are commendable and should be multiplied. However, less structured opportunities are also needed for people who are not aware of their potential for expression. Groups wherein spontaneous handling of whatever medium the person wishes to use to express what he feels enable him to discover some of his own possibilities. In this way also he is opened to an appreciation of those who share this experience with him.

Much is required here if new modes of communication and understanding are to be fostered between person and person. R. D. Laing puts the problem this way:

> The inner does not become outer, and the outer become inner, just by the discovery of the "inner" world. *That is only the beginning.* As a whole generation of men, we are so estranged from the inner world that there are many arguing that it does not exist; and that even if it does exist, it does not matter.[1]

If this is true, and we see evidence that it is, then some concerted effort to comprehend the inner as well as the outer and to get them together is desperately in order.

A serious look at the process of change will show that it is

[1] *The Politics of Experience and the Bird of Paradise* (New York: Ballantine Books, 1967), p. 46. Italics added.

not enough for a person to get insight into himself and his problems. Not even occasional experiencing of other people in groups is sufficient to produce deep transformation. If he cannot translate what he learns and what he feels into effective action in liberating and facilitating community organizations, he is yet incomplete. If he can make a difference in real life, he is making the connection between the inner and the outer. We say he is "coming out somewhere" in strength, not just getting private satisfaction from his experiences of intimacy.

There is no real growth—there is no real development—in the organization or in the individuals within it if they do not confront and deal directly with their problems. They can get together and share feelings, but if that is all they do, it is merely a catharsis. While this is useful, it has relatively minimal usefulness compared with what can happen if they start to relate differently within the organizational setting around task issues.[2]

A distinguishing mark of health in any community organization is lively transaction among the people in it. People who are affected by decisions should participate in the decision-making process. The person who enjoys the freedom to enter responsibly with others in setting up ground rules for their work and play together usually feels responsible to the group. His participation in decision-making not only enhances his self-esteem, but also adds strength to the group of which he is a part.

The culture of an organization is improved when the people in it engage in straightforward but sensitive transactions with each other. Once they realize they can improve that culture by drawing out each other's strengths, rather than engaging in "put downs" to grab control, they can arrive at real solutions to their problems. Their feelings are available to each other. They are open and explicit in their confrontation. However, they do this in the spirit of caring. Confrontation without car-

[2] Sheldon A. Davis, "An Organic Problem-Solving Method of Organizational Change," *The Journal of Applied Behavioral Science*, III (1967), 2.

ing can have the opposite effect; it can destroy rather than fulfill.

The truly significant and enduring changes in any organization, giving it new life, are transformations of the cultural system itself. If an organization is to fulfill the people who make it up, its minisystems, values, processes, norms, and compensations cannot go unchallenged; the very view of the world from which that cultural system gets its meaning must be examined.

Changes in the cultural systems of our organizations and institutions will be in a positive direction if we can manifest our belief in the people in them. The urge for control of people shows up a basic disbelief in them. If we really believe that people have potential, that they are strong, and that they want to make a difference in what goes on in the world, we will act accordingly. We will confront them, support them, give them demanding responsibility, honestly and fairly criticize them, encourage them, and commend them on their accomplishments in growth.

In this way each upbuilds the other and draws strength from the other's strength. Both have become transformed in the process. The whole community experiences transformation as a result! Freeing people to engage in this process is the central task of a community dedicated to liberating and facilitating personal growth.

We began this book by noting modern man's tragic alienation. We cited several cultural analysts who have traced this problem to reductionist views which desensitize man. The reigning scientific world view contributes to that reductionism. While this world view elevates man's capacity to manipulate and control his environment, it cuts him off from the rich world of fantasy and feeling, which makes him truly human. Thus he has learned to master but not to create in the real sense. What we mean by creation is to appreciate and bring out the essence of the other, whatever that other is, whether a person or thing.

We have observed that man's "love affair" with his objective consciousness tends to blind him to his relatedness to all things. He separates himself from the objects of which he is conscious. The tragedy of the separation is the insensitivity which develops. He loses the capacity for empathy. Once he reduces the objects of his consciousness to categories which he can manage, he relates to them in those terms, ignoring other dimensions of the world in which he seeks to become a person.

We have recognized that a revolution in personal consciousness in taking place. For example, young people are vigorously affirming personal values. We have cited spokesmen for the counter-culture revolution, who have articulated the nature of human and personal values. We have said that this revolution is basic to that which is taking place in our social institutions.

A revised world view is essential to giving perspective and vitality to personal and social transformations. The emerging world view will be more inclusive—not scornful of the myths and fantasies which richly fulfill every person's image of himself. It will be appropriately cognizant of the mystery of being and less prone to reduce being to categories which are easily but grossly compartmentalized.

We believe that the changing world view draws vitality and energy from hope generated by Christian faith. Faith which sees man's possibilities in a dying and rising Lord who cannot be restrained by systems or defeated even by death is the essential core of a liberating and facilitating community. Such a community embodies that faith—gives it concrete expression through its own incarnation. We are the "body of Christ." Then let us truly be such a body! Let us sensitize our persons to each other and overcome this fatal alienation in the world. In the household of God we are no longer strangers, sojourners, or aliens, but fellow citizens.

Index

Date Due

Code 4386-04, CLS-4, Broadman Supplies, Nashville, Tenn.,
Printed in U.S.A.